Czech

phrase book &

Dvorak
Smetena
Jonacek
...ka

Berlitz Publishing
New York London Singapore

Contacting the Editors
Every effort has been made to provide accurate information in this publication, but changes are inevitable. The publisher cannot be responsible for any resulting loss, inconvenience or injury. We would appreciate it if readers would call our attention to any errors or outdated information. We also welcome your suggestions; if you come across a relevant expression not in our phrase book, please contact us at: **comments@berlitzpublishing.com**

All Rights Reserved
© Apa Digital (CH) AG and Apa Publications (UK) Ltd
Berlitz Trademark Reg. U.S. Patent Office and other countries. Marca Registrada. Used under license from Berlitz Investment Corporation.

Fourth Printing: 2014
Printed in China

Publishing Director: Agnieszka Mizak
Senior Commissioning Editor: Kate Drynan
Translation: updated by ALINGUA
Simplified phonetics: updated by Wordbank
Cover & Interior Design: Beverley Speight
Production Manager: Vicky Glover
Picture Researcher: Pawel Pasternak
Cover Photos: © iStockphoto; Rod Purcell 'Information Signpost' photo

Interior Photos: APA Rod Purcell 12, 54, 102, 112, 115, 116, 128, 178; iStockphoto 30, 49, 51, 53, 64, 72, 82, 88, 94, 98, 104, 106, 124, 127, 131, 132, 134, 137, 138, 140, 142, 146, 148, 150, 153, 154, 159, 161, 162, 182; APA Corrie Wingate 110, 144; APA A Nowitz 78; APA Lydia Evans 69, 81

Contents

Food & Drink

People

Leisure Time

Special Requirements

In an Emergency

Dictionary

Pronunciation

This section is designed to make you familiar with the sounds of Czech using our simplified phonetic transcription. You'll find the pronunciation of the Czech letters and sounds explained below, together with their "imitated" equivalents. To use this system, found throughout the phrase book, simply read the pronunciation as if it were English, noting any special rules below.

Stress in Czech falls on the first syllable of a word, though it is not as pronounced as in English. Prepositions in Czech are generally pronounced together with their object as a single word, so the stress falls on the preposition:

Example:

Kolik to stojí na den? _koh_•lihk toh' _stoh_•yee _nah_•dehn

How much is it per day?

Consonants

Letter	Approximate Pronunciation	Symbol	Example	Pronunciation
c	like ts in cats	**ts**	**cesta**	_tsehs_•tah
č	like ch in church	**ch**	**klíč**	_kleech_
ch	like ch in the Scottish loch	**kh**	**chyba**	_khih_•bah
ď	like d + y	**dy**	**láďa**	_lah_•dya
g	like g in good	**g**	**galerie**	_gah_•leh•rih•yeh
j	like y in yes	**y**	**jídlo**	_yeeh_•dloh
ň	like ny in canyon; the apostrophe indicates a softening of the sound	**n'**	**píseň**	_peeh_•sehn'

Vowels in Czech marked with ´ are long vowels; these should be lengthened when pronounced. The length of the vowel is an essential feature since it can differentiate the meaning of words that are otherwise written with the same spelling.

Throughout this book, long vowels in the pronunciation column are marked with bold.

ř	like r + zh, run together	**rzh**	**řepa**	_rzheh•pah_
r	as in English, but rolled	**r**	**ruka**	_roo•kah_
s	like s in seat	**s**	**sobota**	_soh•boh•tah_
š	like sh in short	**sh**	**šest**	_shehst_
ť	like tu in tune; the apostrophe indicates a softening of the sound	**t'**	**chuť**	_khoot'_

Czech is a Slavic language, closely related to Slovak, Russian, Polish and Bulgarian. However, unlike Russian and Bulgarian, Czech uses the Roman alphabet. Many Czech and English words have a common origin in Latin, for example: **bratr** (brother) and **sestra** (sister). Czech is a highly inflected language. This means that word endings change to indicate grammatical functions such as gender, number, case, etc.

v	like v in vest	v	**víno**	_vee_·noh
w	found in foreign words only	v	**watt**	_vaht_
z	like z in zoo	z	**zázemí**	_zah_·zeh·m**ee**
ž	like s in pleasure	zh	**žena**	_zheh_·nah

Letters **b, d, f, h, k, l, m, n, p, t, v** are generally pronounced as in English.

Vowels

Letter	Approximate Pronunciation	Symbol	Example	Pronunciation
a	like a in father	ah	**tady**	_tah_·dih
á	like a in father, but longer	ah	**máma**	_mah_·mah
e	like e in met	eh	**den**	dehn
é	like e in met, but longer	eh	**mléko**	m_leh_·koh
i/y	like i in bit	ih	**pivo**	_pih_·voh
í/ý	like ee in see	ee	**bílý**	_bee_·lee
o	like o in hotel	oh	**slovo**	_sloh_·voh
ó	like o in hotel, but longer	oh	**gól**	gohl
u	like oo in book	oo	**ruka**	_roo_·kah
ú/ů	like oo in book, but longer	oo	**úkol, vůz**	_oo_·kol, v_oo_s

Diphthongs

Letter	Approximate Pronunciation	Symbol	Example	Pronunciation
au	like ow in cow	ow	**auto**	_ow_·toh
ou	like the exclamation oh	oh	**mouka**	_moh_·kah

How to use this Book

Sometimes you see two alternatives in italics, separated by a slash. Choose the one that's right for your situation.

ESSENTIAL

I'm here on vacation [holiday]/business.

Jsem zde na dovolené/služebně. *yeh•sem zdeh nah•doh•voh•leh•neh/sloo•zhehb•nyeh*

I'm going to...

Jedu do... *Yeh•doo doh...*

I'm staying at the...Hotel.

Ubytoval m/Ubytovala f jsem se v hotelu... *oo•bih•toh•vahl/oo•bih•toh•vah•lah ysehm se fhoh•teh•loo...*

Words you may see are shown in YOU MAY SEE boxes.

YOU MAY SEE...

K NÁSTUPIŠTÍM	to the platforms
INFORMACE	information
REZERVACE	reservations

Any of the words or phrases listed can be plugged into the sentence below.

Trains

Where is/are...?
   the ticket office
   the information desk
   the luggage lockers

Kde je/jsou...? *gdeh yeh/ysoh...*
pokladna *poh•klahd•nah*
informace *ihn•fohr•mah•tseh*
schránky na zavazadla *shrahn•kih nah zah•vah•zah•dlah*

Czech phrases appear in purple.

Read the simplified pronunciation as if it were English. For more on pronunciation, see page 7.

Tickets

Can I buy a ticket on the bus/train?

Mohu si koupit jízdenku v autobusu/ve vlaku?
moh•hoo sih koh•piht yeez•dehn•koo fow•toh•boo•soo/vehvlah•koo

I'd like to…my reservation.

Chtěl m/Chtěla f bych…moji rezervaci.
khtyehl•khtyeh•lah bihkh…moh•yih reh•zehr•vah•tsih

cancel
change
confirm

zrušit *zroo•shiht*
změnit *zmyeh•niht*
potvrdit *poh•tfr•diht*

For Numbers, see page 175.

Related phrases can be found by going to the page number indicated.

When different gender forms apply, the masculine form is followed by *m*; feminine by *f*.

At some banks, cash can be obtained from ATMs with Visa, Eurocard, American Express and many other international cards. Instructions are often given in English. You can also change money at travel agencies and hotels, but the rate will not be as good.

Information boxes contain relevant country, culture and language tips.

Expressions you may hear are shown in You May Hear boxes.

YOU MAY HEAR…

Jakými aerolinkami letíte?
yah•kee•mih ah•eh•roh•lihn•kah•mih leh•tee•teh

What airline are you flying?

Color-coded side bars identify each section of the book.

Survival

Arrival & Departure

ESSENTIAL

I'm here on vacation [holiday]/business.	**Jsem zde na dovolené/služebně.** *ysehm zdeh <u>nah</u>•doh•voh•leh•n**eh**/<u>sloo</u>•zhehb•nyeh*
I'm going to...	**Jedu do...** *Yeh•doo doh...*
I'm staying at the...Hotel.	**Ubytoval** *m***/Ubytovala** *f* **jsem se v hotelu...** *<u>oo</u>•bih•toh•vahl/<u>oo</u>•bih•toh•vah•lah ysehm se fhoh•teh•loo...*

YOU MAY HEAR...

Letenku/Cestovní pas, prosím. *<u>leh</u>•tehn•koo/<u>tsehs</u>•tohv•n**ee** pahs <u>proh</u>•seem*	Your ticket/passport, please.
Jaký je účel vaší cesty? *<u>yah</u>•k**ee** yeh **oo**•chehl <u>vah</u>•sh**ee** <u>tseh</u>•stih*	What's the purpose of your visit?
Kde jste ubytovaný? *gdeh ysteh <u>oo</u>•bih•toh•vah•n**ee***	Where are you staying?
Jak dlouho tady budete? *yahk <u>dloh</u>•hoh <u>tah</u>•dih boo•deh•teh*	How long are you staying?
S kým tady jste? *sk**ee**m <u>tah</u>•dih ysteh*	Who are you with?

Border Control

I'm just passing through.	**Pouze projíždím.** *<u>poh</u>•zeh proh•y**ee**zh•d**ee**m*

YOU MAY HEAR...

Máte něco k proclení? _mah_·teh _nyeh_·tsoh
kproh·tsleh·n**ee**

Za tohle musíte platit clo. zah _toh_·leh
moo·s**ee**·teh _plah_·tiht tsloh

Otevřte laskavě tuhle tašku/kufr.
_oh_·teh·vrzhteh lahs·kah·vyeh _too_·hleh
tahsh·koo/koofr

Do you have anything to declare?

You must pay duty on this.

Please open this bag/ suitcase.

I would like to declare...	**Rád** m/**Ráda** f **bych přihlásil** m/ **přihlásila** f **k proclení...** _raht/rah_·dah bihkh _przhih_·hl**ah**·sihl/przhih·hl**ah**·sih·lah _kproh_·tsleh·n**ee**...
I have nothing to declare.	**Nemám nic k proclení.** _neh_·m**ah**m nihts _kproh_·tsleh·n**ee**

YOU MAY SEE...

CELNÍ PROHLÍDKA	customs
ZBOŽÍ CLA PROSTÉ	duty-free goods
ZBOŽÍ K PROCLENÍ	goods to declare
NIC K PROCLENÍ	nothing to declare
PASOVÁ KONTROLA	passport control
POLICIE	police

Money

ESSENTIAL

Where's…?	**Kde je…?** *gdeh yeh…*
the ATM	**bankomat** *bahn•koh•maht*
the bank	**banka** *bahn•kah*
the currency exchange office	**směnárna** *smyeh•nahr•nah*
What time does the bank open/close?	**V kolik otvírají/zavírají banku?** *fkoh•lihk oht•fee•rah•yee/zah•vee•rah•yee bahn•koo*
I'd like to change dollars/pounds into crowns.	**Chtěl** *m*/**Chtěla** *f* **bych si vyměnit dolary/libry na koruny.** *khtyehl/khtyeh•lah bihkh sih vih•myeh•niht doh•lah•rih/lihb•rih nah•koh•roo•nih*
I'd like to cash some travelers checks [cheques].	**Chtěl** *m*/**Chtěla** *f* **bych si vyměnit cestovní šeky.** *khtyehl/khtyeh•lah bihkh sih vih•myeh•niht tsehs•tohv•nee sheh•kih*

At the Bank

Can I exchange currency here?	**Mohu si tady vyměnit peníze?** *moh•hoo sih tah•dih vih•myeh•niht peh•nee•zeh*
What's the exchange rate?	**Jaký je kurz?** *yah•kee yeh koors*

YOU MAY SEE…

The monetary unit is the **Česká koruna, Kč** (Czech crown), plural **korun**, which is divided into 100 **haléřů, h.**

Coins: 10, 20 and 50 **h**; 1, 2, 5, 10 and 20 **Kč**

Notes: 20, 50, 100, 200, 500, 1000, 2000 and 5000 **Kč**

15

YOU MAY SEE...

VLOŽTE KARTU	insert card
STORNO	cancel
OPRAVA	clear
ZADEJTE PIN	enter PIN
BĚŽNÝ ÚČET	from checking [current account]
ZŮSTATEK	from savings account
STVRZENKA	receipt

How much is the fee?	**Kolik si účtujete provizi?** _koh_•lihk sih _ooch_•too•yeh•teh _proh_•vih•zih
I've lost my travelers checks [cheques].	**Ztratil m/Ztratila f jsem cestovní šeky.** _strah_•tihl/_strah_•tih•lah ysehm _tsehs_•tohv•nee _sheh_•kih
My card was lost.	**Ztratil m/Ztratila f jsem kartu.** _strah_•tihl/_strah_•tih•lah ysehm _kahr_•too
My credit cards have been stolen.	**Ukradli mi kreditní karty.** _oo_•krahd•lih mih _kreh_•diht•nee _kahr_•tih
My card doesn't work.	**Moje karta nefunguje.** _moh_•yeh _kahr_•tah _neh_•foon•goo•yeh

For Numbers, see page 175.

Banky (banks) are generally open Monday through Friday from 8 a.m. to 5 p.m. with a one-hour lunch break around noon. ATMs are available at most banks, but a commission is charged upon cash withdrawal. **Směnárne** (currency exchange offices) operate in large towns and cities. They are usually open from Monday to Friday from 8 a.m. to 6 p.m. with a one-hour break around noon.

ESSENTIAL

How do I get to town?	**Jak se odtud dostat do mešta?** yahk seh <u>ohd</u>•tood <u>dohs</u>•taht doh <u>meh</u>•shtah
Where's...?	**Kde je...?** gdeh yeh...
the airport	**letiště** <u>leh</u>•tihsh•tyeh
the train station	**nádraží** <u>nah</u>•drah•zh**ee**
the bus station	**autobusové nádraží** <u>ow</u>•toh•boo•soh•veh <u>nah</u>•drah•zh**ee**
the subway [underground] station	**stanice metra** <u>stah</u>•nih•tseh <u>meht</u>•rah
How far is it?	**Jak je to daleko?** yahk yeh toh <u>dah</u>•leh•koh
Where can I buy tickets?	**Kde si mohu koupit jízdenku?** gdeh sih <u>moh</u>•hoo <u>koh</u>•piht <u>yeez</u>•dehn•koo
A one-way [single] ticket.	**Jedním směrem.** <u>yehd</u>•neem <u>smyeh</u>•rehm
A round-trip [return] ticket.	**Zpáteční.** <u>spah</u>•tehch•nee
How much?	**Kolik?** <u>koh</u>•lihk
Are there any discounts?	**Jsou nějaké slevy?** ysoh <u>nyeh</u>•yah•keh <u>sleh</u>•vih
Which gate/ platform?	**Který východ/nástupiště?** kteh•**ree** <u>vee</u>•khohd/<u>nahs</u>•too•pihsh•tyeh
Which line?	**Která linka?** <u>kteh</u>•**rah** lihn•kah
Where can I get a taxi?	**Kde najdu taxík?** gdeh <u>nahy</u>•doo tah•ks**ee**k
Please take me to this address.	**Dovezte mě laskavě na tuhle adresu.** <u>doh</u>•vehs•teh myeh <u>lahs</u>•kah•vyeh nah <u>too</u>•hleh <u>ahd</u>•reh•soo
A map please.	**Prosím mapu.** <u>proh</u>•seem <u>mah</u>•poo

Tickets

When's…to Prague?	**V kolik je…do Prahy?** _fkoh_·lihk yeh…doh _prah_·hih
the (first) bus	**(první) autobus** (prvnee) ow·toh·boos
the (next) flight	**(další) let** (_dahl_·shee) leht
the (last) train	**(poslední) vlak** (_pohs_·lehd·nee) vlahk
Where can I buy	**Kde si mohu koupit jízdenku/letenku?**
train/plane tickets?	gdeh sih _moh_·hoo koh·piht _yeez_·dehn·koo/_leh_·tehn·ko
One/Two ticket(s)	**Prosím jednu jízdenku/dvě jízdenky.**
please.	Proh·seem yed·nu _yeez_·den·koo
For today/tomorrow.	**Na dnešek/zítřek.** nah _dneh_·shehk/zee·trzhehk
…plane/train ticket.	**Letenka/Jízdenka…** _leh_·tehn·kah/
	yeez·dehn·kah…
A one-way	**jedním směrem** _yehd_·neem _smyeh_·rehm
A return trip	**zpáteční** _spah_·tehch·nee
A first class	**do první** _doh_·prvnee
business class	**Třída business** Trzee·dah biz·niss klahs
An economy class	**ekonomické třídy** _eh_·koh·noh·mihts·keh _trzhee_·dih
How much?	**Kolik?** _koh_·lihk
Is there a discount	**Je sleva pro…?** yeh _sleh_·vah proh…
for…?	
children	**děti** _dyeh_·tih
students	**studenty** _stoo_·dehn·tih
senior citizens	**starší občany** _stahr_·shee _ohp_·chah·nih
tourists	**turisté** too·riss·teh
The express bus/	**Prosím jízdenku na dálkový autobus/rychlík.**
express train, please.	Proh·seem yeez·den·koo nah dahl·ko·vee
	ah·oo·toh·boos/rih·khleek
The local bus/train,	**Prosím jízdenku na místní autobus/osobní vlak.**
please.	Proh·seem yeez·den·koo nah meest·nyee
	ah·oo·toh·boos/os·ob·nee vlahk

YOU MAY HEAR...

Další! _dahl·shee_ — Next!

Letenku/Cestovní pas, prosím. _leh·tehn·koo/tsehs·tohv·nee pahs proh·seem_ — Your ticket/passport, please.

Kolik máte zavazadel? _koh·lihk mah·teh zah·vah·zah·dehl_ — How much luggage do you have?

Máte nadváhu. _mah·teh nahd·vah·huh_ — You have excess luggage.

Tohle je na příruční zavazadlo příliš těžké/velké. _toh·hleh yeh nah przhee·rooch·nee zah·vah·zahd·loh przhee·lihsh tyezh·keh/vehl·keh_ — That's too heavy/large for a carry-on [to carry on board].

Balil jste tato zavazadla sám? _bah·lihl ysteh tah·toh zah·vah·zah·dlah sahm_ — Did you pack these bags yourself?

Dal vám někdo nějaké zavazadlo k převezení? _dahl vahm nyehg·doh nyeh·yah·keh zah·vah·zah·dloh kprzheh·veh·zeh·nee_ — Did anyone give you anything to carry?

Vyndejte všechno z kapes, prosím. _vihn·dehy·teh fsheh·khnoh skah·pehs proh·seem_ — Please empty your pockets.

Zujte si boty, prosím. _zooy·teh sih boh·tih proh·seem_ — Take off your shoes, please.

Zveme vás na palubu letadla... _zveh·meh vahs nah pah·loo·boo leh·tahd·lah..._ — Now boarding flight...

I have an e-ticket. — **Mám elektronický lístek.** _mahm eh·lehk·troh·nihts·kee lees·tehk_

Can I buy a ticket on the bus/train? — **Mohu si koupit jízdenku v autobusu/ve vlaku?** _moh·hoo sih koh·piht yeez·dehn·koo fow·toh·boo·soo/ veh vlah·koo_

In Czech, there are different words used for "ticket", depending on how you are traveling. **Letenka** is used for plane tickets and **jízdenka** for train or bus tickets. The generic **lístek** describes all tickets but is rarely used.

Can I buy the ticket before boarding?	**Mohu si koupit jízdenku před nastoupením do autobusu/vlaku?** *moo•hoo sih koh•piht yeez•dehn•koo przed nas•toe•pe•nyeem doh ah•oo•toh•boo•soo/vlah•koo*
How long is this ticket valid?	**Jak dlouho platí jízdenka?** *Yahk dloe•hoh plah•tyee yeez•den•kah?*
Can I return on the same ticket?	**Platí stejná jízdenka i pro zpáteční jízdu?** *Plah•tyee stay•nah yeez•den•kah ee proh spaa•tetch•nyee yeez•doo?*
I'd like to...my reservation.	**Chtěl m/Chtěla f bych...moji rezervaci.** *khtyehl m/khtyeh•lah bihkh...moh•yih reh•zehr•vah•tsih*
cancel	**zrušit** *zroo•shiht*
change	**změnit** *zmyeh•niht*
confirm	**potvrdit** *pohtfr•diht*

For Days, see page 177.

YOU MAY HEAR...

Jakými aerolinkami letíte? *yah•kee•mih ah•eh•roh•lihn•kah•mih leh•tee•teh*	What airline are you flying?
Vnitrostátní nebo mezinárodní? *vnih•troh•staht•nee neh•boh meh•zih•nah•rohd•nee*	Domestic or international?
Který terminál? *kteh•ree tehr•mih•nahl*	What terminal?

YOU MAY SEE...

PŘÍLETY	arrivals
ODLETY	departures
VÝDEJ ZAVAZADEL	baggage claim
VNITROSTÁTNÍ	domestic flights
MEZINÁRODNÍ	international flights
REGISTRACE	check-in desk
ODBAVENÍ S ELEKTRONICKOU JÍZDENKOU	e-ticket check-in
VÝCHODY	departure gates

Plane

Airport Transfer

How much is a taxi to the airport?	**Kolik stojí taxík na letiště?** _koh_·lihk _stoh_·yee _tah_·ks_eek_ _nah_·leh·tihsh·tyeh
To...Airport, please.	**Na letiště..., prosím.** _nah_·leh·tihsh·tyeh _proh_·s_eem_
My airline is...	**Letím aerolinkami...** _leh_·t_eem_ _ah_·eh·roh·lihn·kah·mih...
My flight leaves at...	**Moje letadlo odlétá v...** _moh_·yeh _leh_·tahd·loh _ohd_·_leh_·tah f...
I'm in a rush.	**Mám naspěch.** mahm _nahs_·pyehkh
Can you take an alternate route?	**Můžete jet jinou cestou?** _moo_·zheh·teh yeht _yih_·noh _tsehs_·toh
Can you drive faster/slower?	**Můžete jet rychleji/pomaleji?** _moo_·zheh·teh yeht _rih_·khleh·yih/_poh_·mah·leh·yih

For Time, see page 177.

Checking In

Where is the check-in desk for flight…?	**U které přepážky se odbavuje let…?** *oo·kteh·reh przheh·pah·zhkih seh ohd·bah·voo·yeh leht…*
My name is…	**Jmenuji se…** *ymeh·noo·yih seh…*
I'm going to…	**Jedu do…** *yeh·doo doh…*
I have…	**Mám…** *Maahm…*
one suitcase	**jedno zavazadlo** *yed·noh zah·vah·zah·dloh*
two suitcases	**dvě zavazadla** *dvyeh zah·vah·zah·dlah*
one piece of hand baggage	**jedno příruční zavazadlo** *yed·noh przee·rootch·nyee zah·vah·zah·dloh*
How much luggage is allowed?	**Kolik zavazadel si můžu vzít?** *koh·lihk zah·vah·zah·dehl sih moo·zhoo vzeet*
Is that pounds or kilos?	**Je to vyjádřeno v librách nebo kilogramech?** *Yeh toh vee·yaah·drzeh·noh v lib·raahkh neh·boh kih·loh·grah·mehkh?*
Which terminal?	**Který terminál?** *Kteh·ree ter·mih·naahl?*
Which gate does flight…leave from?	**Z kterého východu linka…odlétá?** *skteh·reh·hoh vee·khoh·doo lihn·kah…ohd·leh·tah*
I'd like a window/ an aisle seat.	**Chtěl m/Chtěla f bych místo u okna/uličky.** *khtyehl/khtyeh·lah bihkh mees·toh oo ohk·nah/ oo·lihch·kih*

YOU MAY SEE…

K NÁSTUPIŠTÍM	platforms
INFORMACE	information
REZERVACE	reservations
PŘÍLETY	arrivals
ODLETY	departures

České dráhy (Czech state-owned railway) offers several transportation options. **Osobní vlak (Os)** (passenger train), stops at every station and operates usually from Monday to Friday, particularly in the morning and early afternoon. **Rychlík (R)** (express train), stops at selected stations, offers first and second-class seating and sometimes also a **jídelní vůz** (restaurant car). **Intercity (IC)** and **Eurocity (EC)** ensure good traveling conditions: air-conditioned first- and second-class cars and a restaurant car. Night trains offer sleeping cars (first class) and couchettes (second class). Trains adapted for disabled persons and bicycles are specially marked.
Since not all ticket offices (especially in smaller towns) accept credit cards, it is advisable to have cash handy.

When do we leave/arrive?	**V kolik to odlétá/přistává?** _fkoh_·lihk toh _ohd_·**leh**·tah/_przhihs_·**tah**·vah
Is the flight... delayed?	**Let...má zpoždění?** leht... mah _spohzh_·dyeh·nee
How late will it be?	**Jaké bude mít zpoždění?** _yah_·**keh** _boo_·deh meet _spohzh_·dyeh·nee

Luggage

Where is/are...?	**Kde je/jsou...?** gdeh yeh/ysoh...
the luggage carts [trolleys]	**vozíky** _voh_·zee·kih
the luggage lockers	**schránky na zavazadla** _shrahn_·kih nah _zah_·vah·zahd·lah
the baggage claim	**výdej zavazadel** _vee_·dehy _zah_·vah·zah·dehl
My luggage has been lost.	**Ztratil m/Ztratila f se mi zavazadla.** _strah_·tihl/_strah_·tih·lah seh mih _zah_·vah·zah·dlah

My luggage has been stolen.	**Někdo mi ukradl zavazadla.**
	nyehg·doh mih <u>ook</u>·rahdl <u>zah</u>·vah·zah·dlah
My suitcase was damaged.	**Můj kufr je poškozený.** _mooy koofr yeh <u>poh</u>·shkoh·zeh·**nee**_

Finding Your Way

Where is/are...?	**Kde je/jsou...?** _gdeh yeh/ysoh..._
the currency exchange office	**směnárna** _smyeh·**nahr**·nah_
the car hire	**půjčovna aut** _<u>pooy</u>·chohv·nah owt_
the exit	**východ** _<u>vee</u>·khohd_
the taxis	**taxík** _tah·ks**eek**_
Is there...into town?	**Jede do města...?** _<u>yeh</u>·deh doh <u>myeh</u>·stah..._
a bus	**autobusu** _<u>ow</u>·toh·boo·soo_
a train	**vlak** _vlahk_
a Metro [subway]	**metro** _<u>meh</u>·troh_

For Asking Directions, see page 34.

YOU MAY HEAR...

Nastupujte prosím! _<u>nahs</u>·too·pooy·teh <u>proh</u>·s**eem**_	All aboard!
Jízdenky, prosím. _<u>yeez</u>·dehn·kih <u>proh</u>·s**eem**_	Tickets, please.
Musíte přestoupit v... _<u>moo</u>·see·teh <u>przheh</u>·stoh·piht v..._	You have to change at...
Příští zastávka... _<u>przheesh</u>·tee <u>zah</u>·st**ahf**·kah..._	Next stop...

Train

How do I get to the train station?	**Jak se dostanu na nádraží?** *yahk seh <u>doh</u>•stah•noo <u>nah</u>•<u>n</u>ah•drah•zhee*
Is it far?	**Je to daleko?** *yeh toh <u>dah</u>•leh•koh*
Where is/are…?	**Kde je/jsou…?** *gdeh yeh/ysoh…*
the ticket office	**pokladna** <u>poh</u>•klahd•nah
the information desk	**informace** <u>ihn</u>•fohr•mah•tseh
the luggage lockers	**schránky na zavazadla** <u>shrahn</u>•kih nah <u>zah</u>•vah•zah•dlah
the platforms	**nástupiště** <u>nah</u>•stoo•pihsh•tyeh
Could I have a schedule [timetable], please?	**Máte jízdní řád, prosím?** <u>mah</u>•teh <u>yeez</u>•dnee rzhaht <u>proh</u>•seem
How long is the trip?	**Jak dlouho trvá cesta?** *yak <u>dloh</u>•hoh trfah <u>tsehs</u>•tah*
Do I have to change trains?	**Musím přestupovat?** <u>moo</u>•seem <u>przheh</u>•stoo•poh•vaht
Is the train on time?	**Přijede vlak včas?** *Przee•yeh•deh vlahk fchahs*

For Tickets, see page 18.

Departures

Which platform does the train to…leave from?	**Ze kterého nástupiště odjíždí vlak do…?** *zeh <u>kteh</u>•reh•hoh <u>nahs</u>•too•pihsh•tyeh <u>ohd</u>•yeezh•dee vlahk doh…*
Is this the track [platform] to…?	**Jede vlak do…z tohoto nástupiště?** *yeh•deh vlahk do…<u>stoh</u>•hoh•toh <u>nahs</u>•too•pihsh•tyeh*
Where is track [platform]…?	**Kde je…nástupiště?** *gdeh yeh… <u>nahs</u>•too•pihsh•tyeh*
Where do I change for…?	**Kde musím přestoupit na…?** *gdeh <u>moo</u>•seem <u>przheh</u>•stoh•piht nah…*

On Board

Is this seat taken?	**Je tohle místo obsazeno?** *yeh toh·hleh mees·toh ohp·sah·zeh·noh*
I think that's my seat.	**Já myslím, že to je moje místo.** *yah mihs·leem zheh toh yeh moh·yeh mees·toh*
Here's my reservation.	**To je moje rezervace.** *Toh yeh mo·hye reh·zehr·vah·tse*

Bus

Where's the bus station?	**Kde je autobusové nádraží?** *gdeh yeh ow·toh·boo·soh·veh nah·drah·zhee*
How far is it?	**Jak je to daleko?** *yahk yeh toh dah·leh·koh*
How do I get to…?	**Jak se dostanu do…?** *yahk seh doh·stah·noo doh…*
Does the bus stop at…?	**Staví tenhle autobus v…?** *stah·vee tehn·hle ow·toh·boos f…*
Could you tell me when to get off?	**Můžete mi říct, kde mám vystoupit?** *moo·zheh·teh mih rzheetst gdeh mahm vihs·toh·piht*

YOU MAY SEE…

AUTOBUSOVÁ ZASTÁVKA	bus stop, (request) stop
VCHOD/VÝCHOD	enter/exit
ZDE OZNAČTE JÍZDENKU	stamp your ticket here

The Prague subway is comprised of three lines (A, B and C), and links to train stations and the Florenc bus station. You can change between lines at three stops: Muzeum (A and C lines), Můstek (A and B lines) and Florenc (B and C lines). The subway operates daily between 5 a.m. and midnight. Line D will be operational from 2018.

| Do I have to change buses? | **Musím přestupovat?** _moo_•s**ee**m _przhehs_•too•poh•vaht |
| Stop here, please! | **Zastavte tady, prosím!** _zahs_•stahf•teh _tah_•dih _proh_•s**ee**m |

For Tickets, see page 18.

Metro

Where's the nearest Metro [subway] station?	**Kde je nejbližší stanice metra?** gdeh yeh _nehy_•blihzh•sh**ee** _stah_•nih•tseh _meht_•rah
Can I have a map of the Metro [subway], please?	**Mohu dostat plán metra, prosím?** _moh_•hoo _dohs_•taht pl**ah**n _meht_•rah _proh_•s**ee**m
Which line for…?	**Kterou trasou se dostanu do…?** _kteh_•roh _trah_•soh seh _dohs_•tah•noo doh…
Which direction?	**Kterým směrem?** _Kteh_•reem smye•hrehm
Do I have to transfer [change]?	**Musím přestupovat?** Moo•s**ee**m _przeh_•stoo•poh•vaht?
Where do I change for…?	**Kde musím přestoupit na…?** gdeh _moo_•s**ee**m _przheh_•stoh•piht nah…
Is this the right train for…?	**Jede to do…?** _yeh_•deh toh doh…
How many stops to…?	**Kolik je to zastávek do …?** Koh•leek yeh toh _zah_•staa•vehk doh…?
Where are we?	**Kde jsme?** gdeh ysmeh

Tram

| Where's the tram stop? | **Kde najdu zastávku tramvaje?** Kdeh _nay_•doo _zah_•staa•fkoo _trahm_•vah•yeh? |
| A map, please. | **Můžu poprosit o mapu?** _Moo_•zhoo _poh_•proh•sit aw _mah_•poo? |

Larger cities and towns in the Czech Republic have a variety of public transportation options, including trains, buses, trams and trolleys; while Prague also has a subway. Smaller towns usually just have a bus service.

Tickets can be purchased from the driver. Large cities often offer 24-hour tickets for use on all types of public transportation. Night service on buses and trams is available in major metropolitan areas; otherwise, hours of operation are generally from 5 a.m. to 10.30 p.m.

Which line for…?	**Kterou linkou se dostanu do…?** _Kteh_·roe _lin_·koe seh _dos_·tah·noo doh …?
Which direction?	**Kterým směrem?** Kteh·reem smnye·rem?
Do I have to transfer [change]?	**Musím přestupovat?** _Moo_·seem _přeh_·stoo·poh·vaht?
Is this the tram to…?	**Je to tramvaj jedoucí do…?** Yeh toh _trahm_·vaayh _yeh_·doe·tsee doh…?
Where are we?	**Kde jsme?** Kdeh smeh?

Boat

When is the boat to…?	**Kdy odplouvá loď na…?** gdih _ohd_·ploh·**vah** _loh_·dyeh _nah_…
Can I take my car on board?	**Mohu vzít na palubu svoje auto?** _moh_·hoo vz**eet** nah _pah_·loo·boo _sfo_·yeh _ow_·toh

---

YOU MAY SEE…

ZÁCHRANNÝ ČLUN	life boats
ZÁCHRANNÁ VESTA	life jackets

> Though the Czech Republic is landlocked, cruising is popular along rivers and other bodies of water. There are several cruise locations, including Prague, Vltavě River, Lipno and Nové Mlýny dams and Máchovo lake.

What time is the next departure?	**V kolik hodin odplouvá další loď?** _F koh_·lik _hoh_·dyin _od_·ploe·vaah _dahl_·shee lodj?
Can I book a seat/cabin?	**Můžu si rezervovat místo k sezení/kajutu?** _Moo_·zhu sih _reh_·zehr·voh·vaht _mees_·toh k _seh_·zeh·nyee?
How long is the crossing?	**Jak dlouho trvá plavba?** Yahk _dloe_·hoh trvaah _plahv_·bah?

For Time, see page 177.

Taxi

Where can I get a taxi?	**Kde najdu taxík?** gdeh _nahy_·doo _tah_·kseek
Can you send a taxi?	**Můžete objednat taxi?** _Moo_·zhu sih ob·yed·naht _tah_·ksih?
Do you have the number for a taxi?	**Máte číslo na taxi firmu?** _Maah_·teh chee·sloh nah _tah_·ksih _fihr_·moo?
I'd like a taxi now/for tomorrow at…	**Chtěl _m_/Chtěla _f_ bych taxík nyní/zítra v…** khtyehl/_khtyeh_·lah bihkh _tah_·kseek nih·_nee_/_zeet_·rah f…

> Taxi stands are marked with **TAXI** signs. Taxis can also be hailed in the street or reserved by phone.

Please, pick me up at…	**Vyzvedněte mne, prosím, v…** *vihz•vehd•nyeh•teh mneh proh•seem f…*
Take me to…	**Zavezte mě laskavě na…** *zah•vehs•teh myeh lahs•kah•vyeh nah…*
this address	**tuhle adresu** *too•hleh ahd•reh•soo*
the airport	**letiště** *leh•tihsh•tyeh*
the train station	**nádraží** *nah•drah•zhee*
I'm late.	**Mám zpoždění.** *mahm spozh•dyeh•nee*
Can you drive faster/slower?	**Můžete jet rychleji/pomaleji?** *moo•zheh•teh yeht rih•khleh•yih/poh•mah•leh•yih*
Stop/Wait here.	**Zastavwte/Počkejte zde.** *sah•stahf•teh/ pohch•kehy•teh sdeh*

YOU MAY HEAR…

Kam jedeme? *kahm yeh•deh•meh*	Where to?
Jaká adresa? *yah•kah ah•dreh•sah*	What's the address?
Je nutné platit zvláštní noční/letištní příplatek. *Yeh noot•neh plah•tyit zvlaah•shtnyee notch•nyee przee•plah•tek*	There's a nighttime/ airport surcharge.

How much will it cost?	**Kolik to bude stát?** _koh_•lihk toh _boo_•deh st**aht**
You said…crowns.	**Jste říkal…korun.** ysteh _rzhee_•kahl…_koh_•roon
Can I have a receipt?	**Mohli byste mi dát stvrzenku?** _moh_•hlih _bihs_•teh mih d**aht** _stvrzehn_•koo
Keep the change.	**Nechte si drobné.** _nehkh_•teh sih _drohb_•n**eh**

YOU MAY SEE…

BENZÍN	gas [petrol]
BEZOLOVNATÝ	unleaded
SPECIAL	regular
SUPER	premium [super]
NAFTA	diesel

Bicycle & Motorbike

I'd like to hire…	**Chtěl** m/**Chtěla** f **bych si půjčit…** khtyehl/_khtyeh_•lah bihkh sih _pooy_•chiht…
a bicycle	**jízdní kolo** _yeez_•dnee _koh_•loh
a moped	**moped** _moh_•pehd
a motorcycle	**motorku** _moh_•tohr•koo
How much per day/ week?	**Kolik to stojí na den/týden?** _koh_•lik toh _stoh_•yee nah dehn/_teeh_•den
Can I have a helmet/ lock?	**Můžete mi dát přilbu/blokádu?** _moo_•zheh•teh mih d**aht** _przhihl_•boo/_bloh_•k**ah**•doo
I have a puncture/ flat tyre.	**Mám píchlou pneumatiku.** Maahm peeh•khloe pne•hoo•mah•tee•koo

YOU MAY HEAR...

Máte mezinárodní řidičský průkaz?
Maa•hteh meh•zih•naah•rod•nyee rzih•dyitch•skee proo•kahs?

Do you have an international driver's license?

Pas, prosím. *pahs proh•seem*

Your passport, please.

Přejete si pojištění? *Przeh•yeh•teh sih poh•yi•shtye•nyee?*

Do you want insurance?

Platí se záloha... *plah•tee seh zah•loh•hah...*

There is a deposit of...

Tady se podepište. *tah•dih seh poh•deh•pihsh•teh*

Sign here.

Car Hire

Where can I rent a car?	**Kde si mohu půjčit auto?** *gdeh sih moh•hoo pooy•chiht ow•toh*
I'd like to rent...	**Chtěl** *m/***Chtěla** *f***bych si půjčit...** *khtyehl/khtyeh•lah bihkh sih pooy•chiht...*
a 2-/4-door car	**dvoudveřové/čtyřdveřové auto** *dvoh•dveh•rzhoh•veh/chtihrzh•dveh•rzhoh•veh ow•toh*
an automatic	**auto s automatickou převodovkou** *ow•toh sow•toh•mah•tihts•koh przheh•voh•dohf•koh*
a manual car	**Automobil s manuální převodovkou** *Ah•owo•toh•moh•bil s mah•noo•aahl•nyee przeh•voh•doh•fkoe*
a car with air-conditioning	**auto s klimatizací** *ow•toh sklih•mah•tih•zah•tsee*
a car seat	**autosedačka** *ow•toh•seh•dahch•kah*
How much...?	**Kolik stojí...?** *koh•lihk stoh•yee...*
per day/week	**na den/týden** *nah dehn/tee•dehn*

YOU MAY SEE...

STŮJ	stop
DEJ PŘEDNOST V JÍZDĚ	yield
ZÁKAZ STÁNÍ	no parking
JEDNOSMĚRNÝ PROVOZ	one way
PRŮJEZD ZAKÁZÁN	no entry
ZÁKAZ PŘEDJÍŽDĚNÍ	no passing
PŘECHOD PRO CHODCE	pedestrian crossing
KŘIŽOVATKA SE SVĚTELNOU	traffic signal ahead

per kilometer	**za kilometr** _zah_·kih·loh·mehtr
for unlimited mileage	**bez kilometrového limitu** behs _kih_·loh·meht·roh·**veh**·hoh _lih_·mih·tuh
with insurance	**s pojištěním** _spoh_·yihsh·tyeh·neem
Are there any discounts?	**Máte speciální slevy?** _**mah**_·teh _speh_·tsy**ahl**·nee _sleh_·vih

Fuel Station

Where's the nearest gas [petrol] station, please?	**Kde je nejbližší benzínová pumpa, prosím?** _gdeh_ yeh _nehy_·blizh·shee _behn_·zee·noh·**vah** _poom_·pah _proh_·**seem**
Fill it up, please.	**Plnou nádrž, prosím.** _plnoh_ n**ah**drzh _proh_·**seem**
...liters, please.	**...litrů, prosím.** ..._liht_·**roo** _proh_·**seem**
I'll pay in cash/ by credit card.	**Zaplatím v hotovosti/kreditní kartou.** _zah_·plah·**teem** _fhoh_·toh·vohs·tih/_kreh_·diht·nee _**kahr**_·toh

For Numbers, see page 175.

Asking Directions

Is this the right road to…?	**Jedu správně na…?** _yeh_·doo _sprah_·vnyeh nah…
How far is it to…?	**Jak je to daleko do…?** _yahk yeh toh _dah_·leh·koh doh…
Where's…?	**Kde je…?** _gdeh yeh…_
…Street	**ulice…** _oo_·lih·tseh…
this address	**tuhle adresu** _too_·hleh _ahd_·reh·soo
the highway [motorway]	**dálnice** _dahl_·nih·tseh
Can you show me on the map?	**Můžete mi to ukázat na mapě?** _moo_·zheh·teh mih toh _oo_·**kah**·zaht _nah_·mah·pyeh
I'm lost.	**Ztratil** m/**Ztratila** f **jsem se.** _strah_·tihl/_strah_·tih·lah ysehm seh

Parking

Can I park here?	**Můžu zde parkovat?** _moo_·zhoo zdeh _pahr_·koh·vaht
Where is the nearest parking lot [car park]?	**Kde je nejbližší parkoviště?** _gdeh yeh _nehy_·blizh·**shee** _pahr_·koh·vihsh·tyeh
Where is the parking meter?	**Kde najdu víceúrovňové parkoviště?** _Kdeh naa_·ydoo vee·tse·oo·rov·nyoh·veh par·koh·vish·tye?
How much…?	**Kolik…?** _koh_·lihk…
per hour	**na hodinu** _nah_·hoh·dih·noo
per day	**na den** _nah_·dehn
overnight	**přes noc** przhehs nohts

Breakdown & Repair

My car broke down.	**Mám na autě poruchu.** _mahm nah _ow_·tyeh _poh_·roo·khoo
My car won't start.	**Auto nechce nastartovat.** _ow_·toh _nehkh_·tseh _nah_·stahr·toh·vaht

YOU MAY HEAR...

přímo před vámi _przhee_·moh przhehd _vah_·mih — straight ahead

vlevo _vleh_·voh — on the left

vpravo _fprah_·voh — on the right

na rohu/za rohem nah _roh_·hoo/ zah _roh_·hehm — on/around the corner

naproti... _nah_·proh·tih — opposite...

za... zah... — behind...

vedle... _vehd_·leh... — next to...

za zah — after

na sever/na jih _nah_·seh·vehr/_nah_·yihh — north/south

na východ/na západ _nah_·vee·khohd/ _nah_·z**ah**·pahd — east/west

na světlách _nah_·sfyeht·_lah_kh — at the traffic lights

na křižovatce na _krzhih_·zhoh·vaht·tseh — at the intersection

Can you fix it? **Můžete to opravit?** _moo_·zheh·teh toh _ohp_·rah·viht

When will it be ready? **Kdy to bude hotové?** gdih toh _boo_·deh _hoh_·toh·v**eh**

How much will it cost? **Kolik to bude stát?** koh·lihk toh _boo_·deh st**aht**

Accidents

There's been an accident. **Stala se nehoda.** _stah_·lah seh _neh_·hoh·dah

Call an ambulance/ the police. **Zavolejte sanitku/policii.** _zah_·voh·lehy·teh _sah_·niht·koo/_poh_·lih·tsih·yih

Places to Stay

ESSENTIAL

Can you recommend a hotel?	**Který hotel byste mi doporučil?** _kteh_•ree _hoh_•tehl _bihs_•teh mih _doh_•poh•roo•chihl
I have a reservation.	**Objednal m/Objednala f jsem si pokoj.** _ohb_•yehd•nahl/_oh_•byehd•nah•lah ysehm sih _poh_•kohy
My name is…	**Jmenuji se…** _ymeh_•noo•yih seh…
Do you have a room…?	**Máte volný pokoj…?** _mah_•teh _vohl_•ne _poh_•kohy…
for one/two	**jednolůžkový/dvoulůžkový** _yeh_•dnoh•_loozh_•koh•vee/_dvoh_•_loozh_•koh•vee
with a bathroom	**s koupelnou** _skoh_•pehl•noh
with air conditioning	**s klimatizací** _sklih_•mah•tih•zah•tsee
for tonight	**na jednu noc** _nah_•yehd•noo nots
for two nights	**na dvě noce** _nah_•dvyeh _noh_•tseh
for one week	**na týden** _nah_•tee•dehn
How much?	**Kolik?** _koh_•lihk
Do you have anything cheaper?	**Máte něco levnějšího?** _mah_•teh _nyeh_•tsoh _lehv_•nyehy•sh_ee_•hoh
When's check-out?	**V kolik hodin musíme uvolnit pokoj?** _fkoh_•lihk _hoh_•dihn _moo_•see•meh _oo_•vohl•niht _poh_•kohy
Can I leave this in the safe?	**Mohu tohle nechat v sejfu?** _moh_•hoo _toh_•hleh _neh_•khaht _fsehy_•foo
Can I leave my bags here?	**Mohu si zde nechat zavazadla?** moh•hoo sih zdeh _neh_•khaht _zah_•vah•zah•dlah
Can I have the bill/ a receipt?	**Mohu dostat stvrzenku/účet?** _moh_•hoo _dohs_•taht _stvrzehn_•koo/_oo_•cheht
I'll pay in cash/ by credit card.	**Zaplatím v hotovosti/kreditní kartou.** zah•plah•teem _fhoh_•toh•vohs•tih/_kreh_•diht•nee _kahr_•toh

Somewhere to Stay

Can you recommend...?	**Který hotel byste mi doporučil?** _kteh_•**ree** hoh•tehl _bihs_•teh mih _doh_•poh•roo•chihl
a hotel	**hotel** _hoh_•tel
a hostel	**hostel** _hos_•tel
a campsite	**tábořiště** _taah_•boh•rzish•tyeh
a bed and breakfast (B&B)	**hotel typu bed and breakfast (B&B)** _hoh_•tel _tih_•poo bed and breakfast (B&B)
What is it near to?	**Je někde nablízku?** yeh _nyehg_•deh _nah_•blee•skoo
How do I get there?	**Jak se tam dostanu?** yahk seh tahm _dohs_•tah•noo

At the Hotel

I have a reservation.	**Objednal** _m_/**Objednala** _f_ **jsem si pokoj.** _ohb_•yehd•nahl/_oh_•byehd•nah•lah ysehm sih _poh_•kohy
My name is...	**Jmenuji se...** _ymeh_•noo•yih seh...
Do you have a room...?	**Máte volný pokoj...?** _mah_•teh vohl•_nee_ _poh_•kohy...
with a bathroom [toilet]/shower	**s koupelnou/sprchou** s _koh_•pehl•noh/sprkhoh
with air conditioning	**s klimatizací** _sklih_•mah•tih•zah•ts_ee_
A smoking/ non-smoking room, please.	**Pokoj pro kuřáky/nekuřáky, prosím.** _poh_•kohy proh _koo_•rzh_ah_•kih/_neh_•koo•rzh_ah_•kih _proh_•_see_m
for tonight	**na jednu noc** _nah_•yehd•noo nohts
for two nights	**na dvě noce** _nah_•dvyeh _noh_•tseh
for one week	**na týden** _nah_•tee•dehn
Does the hotel have...?	**Je v hotelu...?** yeh _fhoh_•teh•loo...
a computer	**počítač** _poh_•chee•tahch
an elevator [lift]	**výtah** _vee_•tahh
(wireless) internet service	**(bezdrátové) internetové služby** _(behz_•drah•toh•veh) ihn•tehr•neh•toh•veh _sloo_•zhbih

room service	**room service** room <u>sehr</u>·vihs
a swimming pool	**bazén** bah·zehn
a gym	**posilovna** <u>poh</u>·sih·loh·vnah
I need…	**Potřebuji…** <u>poh</u>·trzheh·boo·yih…
an extra bed	**lůžko navíc** <u>loo</u>·shkoh nah·**veets**
a cot	**skládací postel** <u>sklah</u>·dah·tsee <u>pohs</u>·tehl
a crib [child's cot]	**kolébku** <u>koh</u>·<u>lehp</u>·koo

Price

How much per night/week?	**Kolik se platí za noc/týden?** <u>koh</u>·lihk seh <u>plah</u>·tee zah nohts/<u>tee</u>·dehn
Does the price include breakfast/sales tax [VAT]?	**Je v ceně snídaně/DPH?** yeh <u>ftseh</u>·nyeh <u>snee</u>·dah·nyeh/<u>deh</u>·peh·hah
Are there any discounts?	**Nabízíte nějaké slevy?** Nah·bee·zee·teh nye·yah·keh sleh·vy?

For deluxe lodgings, you can expect to pay for them as some of the best hotels in the country are located in grandiose former castles and palaces.

Alternatively, motels can be found in the countryside and along the main highways and are reasonably priced.

Campsites are perfect for nature lovers. In the Czech Republic you'll find them along rivers and by lakes. Cabins need to be booked in advance though, especially during the busy summer months.

Finally, **privát** (private rooms) are the equivalent of bed and breakfasts but facilities do vary.

YOU MAY HEAR...

Váš cestovní pas/kreditní karta, prosím. *vahsh tsehs•tohv•nee pahs/ kreh•diht•nee kahr•tah proh•seem*

Your passport/credit card, please.

Vyplňte, prosím, tento formulář. *vih•pln'teh proh•seem tehn•toh fohr•moo•lahrzh*

Please fill out this form.

Tady se podepište. *tah•dih seh poh•deh•pihsh•the*

Sign here.

Preferences

Can I see the room?	**Můžu vidět pokoj?** *Moo•zhu vih•dyet poh•koy?*	
I'd like a...room.	**Chtěl bych/chtěla bych...pokoj.** *Hkhtyel bihkh/ hkhtye•lah bihkh ... poh•koy.*	
better	**lepší** *lep•shee*	
bigger	**větší** *vyet•shee*	
cheaper	**levnější** *lev•nyey•shee*	
quieter	**tišší** *tyish•shee*	
I'll take it.	**Vezmu si ho.** *Vez•moo sih hoh*	
No, I won't take it.	**Ne, nevezmu si ho.** *Neh, neh•vez•moo sih hoh.*	

Questions

Where's...?	**Kde je...?** *gdeh yeh...*	
the bar	**bar** *bahr*	
the restroom [toilet]	**záchod** *zah•khoht*	
the elevator [lift]	**výtah** *vee•tahh*	
the room	**pokoj** *poh•koy*	
Can I have...?	**Mohu dostat...?** *moh•hoo dohs•taht...*	
a blanket	**přikrývku** *przhih•kreef•koo*	

YOU MAY SEE...

TAM/SEM	push/pull
ZÁCHODY	restroom [toilet]
SPRCHA	shower
VÝTAH	elevator [lift]
SCHODIŠTĚ	stairs
PRODEJNÍ AUTOMATY	vending machines
LED	ice
PRÁDELNÍ SLUŽBA	laundry
NERUŠIT	do not disturb
PROTIPOŽÁRNÍ DVEŘE	fire door
NOUZOVÝ VÝCHOD	emergency exit
BUZENÍ TELEFONEM	wake-up call

	an iron	**žehličku** _zheh_•hlihch•koo
	key/key card	**klíč/kartu do dveří** kleetch/_kahr_•too doh _dveh_•rzee
	a pillow	**polštář** _pohlsh_•tahrzh
	soap	**mýdlo** _mee_•dloh
	toilet paper	**toaletní papír** _toh_•ah•leht•nee _pah_•peer
	a towel	**ručník** _rooch_•neek
Do you have an adapter for this?		**Máte k tomu adapteru?** _mah_•teh _ktoh_•moo _ah_•dahp•teh•roo
How do I turn on the lights?		**Jak se zde zapíná svetlo?** yahk seh zdeh _zah_•pee•nah _sveht_•loh
Could you wake me at…?		**Vzbudili byste mě v…?** _vzboo_•dih•lih _bihs_•teh myeh f…
I'd like my things from the safe.		**Chtěl** m/**Chtěla** f **bych si vyzvednout své věci ze sejfu.** khtyehl/_khtyeh_•lahbihkh sih _vihz_•vehd•noht s_feh_ vyeh•tsih _zeh_•sehy•foo

Is there mail/ a message for me?	**Máte pro mne nějakou poštu/nějaký vzkaz?** _mah_•teh proh mneh _nyeh_•jah•koh _pohsh_•too/ _nyeh_•yah•**kee** fskahz
Do you have a laundry service?	**Máte tady prádelnu?** _Maah_•teh tah•dy praah•dell•noo?

Problems

There's a problem.	**Mám problém.** _mahm_ _prohb_•lehm
I've lost my key/ key card.	**Ztratil** _m_/**Ztratila** _f_ **jsem klíč/klíčovú kartu.** _strah_•tihl/_strah_•tih•lah ysehm kl_ee_ch/_klee_•choh•**voo** _kahr_•too
I've locked myself out of my room.	**Zabouchl** _m_/**Zabouchla** _f_ **jsem si dveře.** _zah_•bohkhl/ _zah_•boh•khlah ysehm sih _dveh_•rzheh
There's no hot water.	**Neteče horká voda.** _neh_•teh•cheh _hohr_•kah _voh_•dah
There's no toilet paper.	**Není tam toaletní papír.** _neh_•nee tahm _toh_•ah•leht•nee _pah_•peer
The room is dirty.	**Pokoj je špinavý.** _poh_•kohy yeh _shpih_•nah•**vee**
There are bugs in our room.	**V našem pokoji jsou hmyzy.** _vnah_•shehm _poh_•koh•yih yhsoh _hmih_•zih
the air conditioning	**klimatizace** _klih_•mah•tih•zah•tseh
the fan	**větrák** _vyeht_•**rah**k
the heat [heating]	**topení** _toh_•peh•nee
the light	**světlo** _svyeht_•loh
the TV	**TV** _tih_•vih
the toilet	**záchod** _zah_•khohd
. . . doesn't work.	**. . . nefunguje.** . . . _neh_•foon•goo•yeh

Hotel staff (doormen, porters and housekeeping personnel) are customarily tipped a few **korun** for service.

Can you fix...?	**Můžete opravit...?** _moo_·zheh·teh _oh_·prah·viht...
I'd like to move to another room.	**Chtel** _m_/**Chtěla** _f_ **bych se přestěhovat do jiného pokoje.** khtyehl/_khtyeh_·lah bihkh seh _przheh_·styeh·hoh·vaht doh _yih_·_neh_·hoh poh·koh·yeh

Electricity in the Czech Republic is 230 volts. You may need a converter and/or an adapter for your appliances.

Checking Out

When's check-out?	**V kolik hodin musíme uvolnit pokoj?** _fkoh_·lihk _hoh_·dihn moo·_see_·meh _oo_·vohl·niht poh·kohy
Could I leave my bags here until...?	**Mohu si tady nechat zavazadla doh...?** _moh_·hoo sih _tah_·dih _neh_·khaht _zah_·vah·zah·dlah doh...
Can I have an itemized bill/a receipt?	**Mohli byste mi účet rozepsat/dát stvrzenku?** _moh_·hlih bihs·teh mih **oo**·cheht _roh_·zehp·saht/d**aht** stvrzehn·koo
I think there's a mistake in this bill.	**Myslím, že v účtu je chyba.** _mihs_·leem zheh **voo**·chtoo yeh _khih_·bah
I'll pay in cash/ by credit card.	**Zaplatím v hotovosti/kreditní kartou.** _zah_·plah·**t**eem _fhoh_·toh·vohs·tih/_kreh_·diht·**nee** kar·toh

Renting

I've reserved an apartment/ a room.	**Objednal** _m_/**Objednala** _f_ **jsem si u vás byt/pokoj.** _ohb_·yehd·nahl/_ohb_·yehd·nah·lah ysehm sih oo v**ahs** biht/_poh_·kohy
My name is...	**Jmenuji se...** _ymeh_·noo·yih seh...
Can I have the key/ key card?	**Mohu dostat klíč/klíčovou kartu?** _moh_·hoo dohs·taht kl**ee**ch/_klee_·choh·**voo** _kahr_·too
Are there sheets?	**Je zde ložní prádlo?** yeh zdeh _lohzh_·nee _prah_·dloh

Are there...?	**Jsou zde...?** *ysoh zdeh...*	
dishes	**nádobí** *nah-doh-bee*	
pillows	**polštáře** *pohl-shtah-rzheh*	
towels	**ručníky** *rooch-nee-kih*	
When/Where do I put out the trash [rubbish]?	**Kdy/Kam odvážejí odpadky?** *gdih/kahm ohd-vah-zheh-yee ohd-pahd-kih*	
When/Where do I put out the recycling?	**Kdy/kde se odevzdávají odpady k recyklaci?** *Kdyh/kdeh seh oh-devz-daah-vah-yee od-pah-dee k reh-tsik-lah-tsi*	
...is broken.	**...nefunguje.** *...neh-foon-goo-yeh*	
How does...work?	**Jak...funguje?** *yahk...foon-goo-yeh*	
the air conditioner	**klimatizace** *klih-mah-tih-zah-tseh*	
the dishwasher	**myčka** *mihch-kah*	
the freezer	**mraznička** *mrahz-nihch-kah*	
the heater	**topení** *toh-peh-nee*	
the microwave	**mikrovlnná trouba** *mih-kroh-vlnah troh-bah*	
the refrigerator	**lednička** *lehd-nihch-kah*	
the stove	**vařič** *vah-rzhihch*	
the washing machine	**pračka** *prahch-kah*	

Domestic Items

I need...	**Potřebuji...** *poh-trzheh-boo-yih...*	
an adapter	**adaptér** *ah-dahp-tehr*	
aluminum [kitchen] foil	**alobal** *ah-loh-bahl*	
a bottle opener	**otvírač na láhve** *oht-fee-rahch nah-lah-hveh*	
a broom	**smetáček** *smeh-tah-chehk*	
a can opener	**otvírač na plechovky** *oht-fee-rahch nah-pleh-khohf-kih*	
cleaning supplies	**čisticí potřeby** *chihs-tih-tsee poht-rzheh-bih*	

a corkscrew	**vývrtku**	_vee_·vrtkoo
detergent	**prášek na praní**	_prah_·shehk _nah_·prah·nee
dishwashing liquid	**prostředek na mytí nádobí**	_prohs_·trzheh·dehk _nah_·mih·**tee** _nah_·doh·bee
garbage [bin] bags	**pytle na odpadky**	_piht_·leh nah·oht·paht·kih
a light bulb	**žárovku**	_zhah_·rohf·koo
matches	**zápalky**	_zah_·pahl·kih
a mop	**mop**	mohp
napkins	**papírové ubrousky**	_pah_·pee·roh·veh _oob_·rohs·kih
paper towels	**papírové ručníky**	_pah_·pee·roh·veh _rooch_·nee·kih
plastic wrap [cling film]	**potravinovou fólii**	_poht_·rah·vih·noh·voh _foh_·lyih
a plunger	**plunžr**	ploonzhr
scissors	**nůžky**	_noosh_·kih
a vacuum cleaner	**vysavač**	_vih_·sah·vahch

For In the Kitchen, see page 72.

At the Hostel

Do you have any places left for tonight?	**Máte na dnes ještě volná místa?**	_mah_·teh _nah_·dnehs _yehsh_·tyeh _vohl_·nah mees·tah
Can I have…?	**Mohu dostat…?**	moh·hoo _dohs_·taht…
a single/	**jednolůžkový**	_yehd_·noh·loozh·koh·vee
double room	**dvoulůžkový pokoj**	dvoh·loozh·koh·vee _poh_·kohy
a blanket	**přikrývku**	_przih_·kreef·koo
pillows	**polštáře**	_pohl_·shtah·rzheh
sheets	**ložní prádlo**	_lohzh_·nee _prah_·dloh
towels	**ručníky**	_rooch_·nee·kih
Do you have lockers?	**Máte uzamykatelné skříňky?**	_Maah_·teh oo·zah·mih·kah·tell·neh skrzeen·ky?
What time do you lock up?	**V kolik hodin se zamyká vchod?**	_fkoh_·lihk _hoh_·dihn seh _zah_·mih·**kah** fkhoht

Youth hostels are popular in the Czech Republic. They usually offer both private and dormitory-style rooms. Being relatively inexpensive, they attract mainly young people and budget travelers. Additional budget accommodations are available; try **vysokoškolské**.

Do I need a membership card?	**Potřebuji členskou kartu?**	*Pot·rzeh·boo·yih jlen·skoe kahr·too?*
Here's my international student card.	**To je moje mezinárodní studentská legitimace.**	*Toh yeh moh·yeh meh·zih·naah·rod·nyee stoo·dent·skaah le·ghi·tih·mah·tseh*

Going Camping

Can I camp here?	**Mohu tady postavit stan?**	*moh·hoo tah·dih pohs·tah·viht stahn*
Is there a campsite	**Je tu nablízku kempink?**	*yeh too nah·blees·koo kehm·pihnk*
What is the charge per day/week?	**Jaký je poplatek za den/týden?**	*yah·kee yeh poh·plah·tehk zah dehn/tee·dehn*
Are there...?	**Je zde...?** *yeh zdeh...*	
cooking facilities	**kuchyňské vybavení** *koo·khihn'·skeh vih·bah·veh·nee*	
electrical outlets	**elektrické zásuvky** *eh·lehk·trihts·keh zah·soof·kih*	
laundry facilities	**prádelna** *prah·dehl·nah*	
showers	**sprchy** *sprkhih*	

YOU MAY SEE...

PITNÁ VODA	drinking water
ZÁKAZ KEMPOVÁNÍ	no camping
ZÁKAZ ROZDĚLÁVÁNÍ OHNĚ/POUŽITÍ GRILU	no fires/barbecues

tents for hire	**možnost si vypůjčit stan** _mohzh_·nohst sih _vih_·**poo**y·chiht stahn
Where can I empty the chemical toilet?	**Kde můžu vyprázdnit chemický záchod?** gdeh _moo_·zhoo vihp·**r**ahzd·niht _kheh_·mihts·k**ee** _zah_·khohd

For Domestic Items, see page 43.

Communications

ESSENTIAL

Is there an internet café nearby?	**Je tady někde nablízku internetová kavárna?** yeh _tah_·dih _nyeg_·deh _na_·bl**ee**s·kuh _ihn_·tehr·neh·toh·**vah** _kah_·**vahr**·nah
How do I connect/ log on?	**Jak se mohu připojit na síť/zalogovat?** yahk seh _moh_·hoo _przhih_·poh·yiht nah s**eet**'/_zah_·loh·goh·vaht
I'd like a phone card.	**Chtěl m/Chtěla f bych telefonní kartu.** khtyehl/_khtyeh_·lah bihkh _teh_·leh·fohn·n**ee** _kahr_·too
Can I have your phone number?	**Dáte mi vaše telefonní číslo?** _dah_·teh mih _vah_·sheh _teh_·leh·fohn·n**ee** _chees_·loh
Here's my number/ e-mail address.	**Tady je moje číslo/emailová adresa.** _tah_·dih yeh _moh_·yeh _chees_·loh/_eh_·mehy·loh·**vah** _ahd_·reh·sah
Call me.	**Zavolejte mi.** _zah_·voh·lehy·teh mih
E-mail me.	**Pošlete mi e-mail.** _poh_·shleh·teh mih _eh_·mehyl
Hello. This is...	**Dobrý den. Tady je...** _dohb_·**ree** dehn _tah_·dih yeh...
I'd like to speak to...	**Chtěl m/Chtěla f bych mluvit s...** khtyehl/_khtyeh_·lah bihkh _mloo_·viht s...
Could you repeat that?	**Můžete to zopakovat?** _moo_·zheh·teh toh _zoh_·pah·koh·vaht

I'll call back later.	**Zavolám později.** _zah_·voh·**lahm** _pohz_·dyeh·yih
Bye.	**Na shledanou.** _nahs_·hleh·dah·noh
Can I access the internet/check e-mail here?	**Mohu zde použit internet/přečíst poštu?** _moh_·hoo zdeh _poh_·zhiht _ihn_·tehr·neht/_przheh_·**cheest** _pohsh_·too
How much per hour/half hour?	**Kolik stojí hodina/půl hodiny?** _koh_·lihk **stoh**·yee _hoh_·dih·nah/**pool** _hoh_·dih·nih
Where's the post office?	**Kde je pošta?** gdeh yeh _pohsh_·tah
I'd like to send this to…	**Chtěl** m/**Chtěla** f **bych to poslat do…** khtyehl/_khtyeh_·lah bihkh toh _pohs_·laht doh…

Online

Where's an internet cafe?	**Kde je internetová kavárna?** gdeh yeh _ihn_·tehr·neh·toh·**vah** _kah_·**vahr**·nah
Does it have wireless internet?	**Je tady bezdrátový internet?** yeh _tah_·dih _behz_·**drah**·toh·**vee** _ihn_·tehr·neht
What is the WiFi password?	**Jaké je heslo pro WiFi?** _Yah_·keh yeh hes·loh proh Wih·Fih?
Is the WiFi free?	**Je WiFi zdarma?** Yeh Wih·Fih zdah·rmah?
Do you have bluetooth?	**Máš bluetooth?** Maash bluetooth?
How do I turn the computer on/off?	**Jak se zapíná/vypíná počítač?** yahk seh _zah_·**pee**·nah/_vih_·**pee**·nah _poh_·**chee**·tahch
Can I…?	**Mohu…?** _moh_·hoo…
access the internet here	**se odtud připojit na internet** seh _oht_·tood _przhih_·poh·yiht nah _ihn_·tehr·neht
check e-mail	**skontrolovat poštu** _skohn_·troh·loh·vaht _pohsh_·too
print	**něco vytisknout** _nyeh_·tsoh _vih_·tihs·knoht
use any computer	**používat počítač** _poh_·oo·zhee·vaht _poh_·**chee**·tahch

plug in/charge my laptop/iPhone/ iPad/BlackBerry?	**si připojit/nabít svůj notebook/iPhone/iPad?** *sih przih·poh·yit/nah·beet svooy notebook/iPhone/iPad?*
How much per hour/ half hour?	**Kolik stojí hodina/půl hodiny?** *koh·lihk stoh·yee hoh·dih·nah/pool hoh·dih·nih*
How do I...?	**Jak se mohu...?** *yahk seh moh·hoo...*
connect/disconnect	**připojit na síť/odpojit** *przhih·poh·yiht nah seet'/ oht·poh·yeet*
log on/off	**zalogovat/vylogovat** *zah·loh·goh·vaht/ vih·loh·goh·vaht*
type this symbol	**zapsat tento symbol** *zahp·saht tehn·toh sihm·bohl*

YOU MAY SEE...

ZAVŘIT	close
ZRUŠIT	delete
E-MAIL	email
UKONČIT	exit
POMOC	help
KOMUNIKÁTOR	instant messenger
INTERNET	internet
LOGIN	login
NOVÝ VZKAZ	new (message)
ZALOGOVAT/VYLOGOVAT	log on/off
ZAPNOUT/VYPNOUT	on/off
OTEVŘIT	open
TISKNOUT	print
CHRÁNIT	save
POSLAT	send
NÁZEV UŽIVATELE/HESLO	username/password
BEZDRÁTOVÝ INTERNET	wireless internet

What's your e-mail?	**Jakou máte emailovou adresu?** _yah_·koh _mah_·teh _eh_·mehy·loh·voh _ahd_·reh·soo
My e-mail is…	**Moje emailová adresa je…** _moh_·yeh _eh_·mehy·loh·**vah** _ahd_·reh·sah yeh…
Do you have a scanner?	**Máte skener?** _Maah_·teh sken·nehr?

Social Media

Are you on Facebook/ Twitter?	**Máš účet na Facebooku/Twitteru?** _Maash oo_·tchet nah Face·boo·koo/Twi·tte·roo?
What's your username?	**Jaké je tvoje uživatelské jméno?** _Yah_·keh yeh tvoh·yeh oo·zhih·vah·tell·skeh ye·meh·noh?
I'll add you as a friend.	**Přidám si tě do přátel.** _Przih_·daahm sih tyeh doh przaah·tell
I'll follow you on Twitter.	**Začnu tě sledovat na Twitteru.** _Zatch_·noo tyeh sleh·doh·vaht nah Twi·tte·roo
Are you following…?	**Sledujete..?** _Sleh_·doo·yeh·teh
I'll put the pictures on Facebook/Twitter.	**Dám fotky na Facebook/Twitter.** _Daam fot_·kih nah Facebook
I'll tag you in the pictures.	**Označím tě na fotkách.** _Oz_·nah·tcheem tyeh nah fot·kaahkh

Phone

A phone card, please.	**Kartu na telefon, prosím.** _kahr_·too _nah_·teh·leh·fohn proh·s**ee**m
A pre-paid phone please.	**Prosím předplacený telefon.** Proh·seem przed·plah·tseh·nee teh·leh·fohn
How much?	**Kolik?** _koh_·lihk
What's the country code for...?	**Jaké je směrovací číslo do...?** _yah_·k**eh** yeh _smyeh_·roh·vah·ts**ee** _chee_·sloh doh...
What's the number for Information?	**Jake je číslo na informaci?** _yah_·keh yeh _chee_·sloh nah _ihn_·fohr·mah·tsih

YOU MAY HEAR...

Promiňte, kdo volá? _proh_·m**ee**n'·tyeh gdoh voh·_lah_	Who's calling, please?
Počkejte chvilku, prosím. _pohch_·kehy·teh khfihl·koo proh·s**ee**m	Hold, please.
Přepojím Vás. _przheh_·poh·y**ee**m vahs	I'll put you through.
Není tu/Je na jiné lince. Nehnyee too/ Yeh nah yih·neh lin·tseh	He/She is not here/on another line.
Chcete ji nechat vzkaz? _khtseh_·teh yih _neh_·khaht fskahs	Would you like to leave a message?
Zavolejte později/za deset minut. _zah_·voh·lehy·teh _pohz_·dyeh·yih/zah _deh_·seht mih·noot	Call back later/in 10 minutes.
Může vám on/ona zavolat? _moo_·zheh vahm ohn/_oh_·nah _zah_·voh·laht	Can he/she call you back?
Jaké je vaše číslo? _yah_·keh yeh _vah_·sheh _chee_·sloh	What's your number?

I'd like the number for...	**Chtěl** *m*/**Chtěla** *f* **bych číslo na...** khtyehl/<u>khtyeh</u>·lah bihkh <u>chee</u>·sloh nah...
My phone doesn't work here.	**Můj telefon zde nefunguje.** *m*ooy teh·leh·fohn zdeh neh·foon·goo·yeh
What network are you on?	**Jakého máš operátora?** Yah·keh·hoh maash o·peh·raah·toh·rah?
Is it 3G?	**Je to 3G?** Yeh toh trzi gheh?
I have run out of credit/minutes.	**Došel mi kredit.** Doh·shell mih kreh·dit
Can I buy some credit?	**Můžu si koupit kredit?** Moo·zhu sih koe·pit kreh·dit?
Do you have a phone charger?	**Máte nabíječku na telefon?** Maa·teh nah·bee·yetch·koo nah teh·leh·fohn?
Here's my number.	**Tady je moje číslo.** <u>tah</u>·dih yeh <u>moh</u>·yeh <u>chees</u>·loh
Can I have your number?	**Dáte mi vaše telefonní číslo?** <u>dah</u>·teh mih <u>vah</u>·sheh teh·leh·foh·<u>nee</u> <u>chees</u>·loh
Call me.	**Zavolejte mi.** <u>zah</u>·voh·lehy·teh mih
Text me.	**Pošlete mi sms-ku.** <u>pohsh</u>·leh·teh mih ehs·ehm·ehs·koo
I'll call you.	**Zavolám vás.** <u>zah</u>·voh·<u>lahm</u> vahs
I'll text you.	**Pošlu vám sms-ku.** <u>pohsh</u>·loo vahm <u>ehs</u>·ehm·ehs·koo

For Numbers, see page 175.

YOU MAY HEAR...

Vyplňte laskavě celní prohlášení. *vihpln'·teh* Please fill out the customs
lahs·kah·vyeh tsehl·nee proh·hlah·sheh·nee declaration form.
Jakou má hodnotu? *yah·koh mah* What's the value?
hohd·noh·too
Co v něm je? *tsoh vnyehm yeh* What's inside?

Telephone Etiquette

Hello. This is...	**Dobrý den. Tady je...** *dohb·ree dehn tah·dih yeh...*	
I'd like to speak to...	**Chtěl** m/**Chtěla** f **bych mluvit s...** *khtyehl/ khtyeh·lah bihkh mloo·viht s...*	
Extension...	**Linka...** *lihn·kah...*	
Speak louder/ more slowly, please.	**Mluvte hlasitěji/pomaleji, prosím.** *mloof·teh hlah·sih·tyeh·yih/poh·mah·leh·yih proh·seem*	
Could you repeat that?	**Můžete to zopakovat?** *moo·zheh·teh toh zoh·pah·koh·vaht*	
I'll call back later.	**Zavolám později.** *zah·voh·lahm pohz·dyeh·yih*	
Bye.	**Na shledanou.** *nahs·hleh·dah·noh*	

Fax

Can I send/receive a fax here?	**Můžu odtud odeslat/zde prijmout fax?** *moo·zhoo ohd·tood oh·dehs·laht/zdeh prihy·moht fahks*
What's the fax number?	**Jaké je číslo faxu?** *yah·keh yeh chee·sloh fahk·soo*
Please fax this to...	**Přefaxujte mi to, prosím, do** *przheh·fah·ksooy·teh mih toh proh·seem doh...*

Post

Where's the post office/mailbox [postbox]?	**Kde je pošta/poštovní schránka?** *gdeh yeh pohsh·tah/pohsh·tohv·nee shrahn·kah*
A stamp for postcard/ letter, please.	**Známku na pohlednici/dopis, prosím.** *znahm·koo nah poh·hlehd·nih·tsih/doh·pihs proh·seem*
How much?	**Kolik?** *koh·lihk*
I want to send this package by airmail/ express.	**Chtel m/Chtěla f bych poslat tento balík letecky/spěšně.** *Khtyehl/khtyeh·lah bihkh pohs·laht tehn·toh bah·leek leh·tehts·kih/spyehsh·nyeh*
A receipt, please.	**Stvrzenku, prosím.** *stvrzehn·koo proh·seem*

Hours of operation for **pošty** (post offices) are: Monday to Friday, 8 a.m. to 5 or 6 p.m.; Saturday, 8 a.m. to noon. In large cities, such as Ostrava or Brno, some post offices have longer hours, while the main post office in Prague is open 24-hours a day, seven days a week. Post offices can also be found in some shopping malls.

Food & Drink

ESSENTIAL

Can you recommend a good restaurant/bar?	**Můžete mi doporučit dobrou restauraci/bar?** *moo*·zheh·teh mih *doh*·poh·roo·chiht *doh*·broh *rehs*·tow·rah·tsih/bahr
Is there a traditional Czech/an inexpensive restaurant near here?	**Je tu někde nablízku tradiční česká/levná restaurace?** yeh too *nyek*·deh *nahb*·lees·koo *trah*·dihch·nee chehs·kah/*lehv*·nah rehs·tow·rah·tseh
A table for..., please.	**Stůl pro..., prosím.** stool proh... *proh*·seem
Could we sit...?	**Mohli bychom si sednout...?** *moh*·hlih *bih*·khohm sih *sehd*·noht...
here/there	**tady/tam** *tah*·dih/tahm
outside	**venku** *vehn*·koo
in a non-smoking area	**v části pro nekuřáky** *fchahs*·tih proh *neh*·koo·rzh**ah**·kih
I'm waiting for someone.	**Čekám někoho.** *cheh*·kahm *nyeh*·koh·hoh
Where are the restrooms [toilets]?	**Kde jsou záchody?** gdeh ysoh *zah*·khoh·dih
A menu, please.	**Jídelní lístek, prosím.** *yee*·dehl·nee *lees*·tehk *proh*·seem
What do you recommend?	**Co nám můžete doporučit?** tsoh nahm *moo*·zheh·the doh·poh·roo·chiht
I'd like...	**Chtěl m/Chtěla f bych...** khtyehl/*khtyeh*·lah bikh...
Some more..., please.	**Ještě trochu..., prosím.** *yehsh*·tyeh *troh*·khoo... *proh*·seem
Enjoy your meal.	**Nechte si chutnat.** *nehkh*·teh sih *khoot*·naht

The check [bill], please.	**Účet, prosím.** _oo_·cheht _proh_·s**ee**m
Is service included?	**Je v tom zahrnutá obsluha?** yeh ftohm
	zah·hrnoo·_tah_ _ohp_·sloo·hah
Can I pay by	**Mohu zaplatit kreditní kartou?** _moh_·hoo
credit card?	zah·plah·tiht _kreh_·diht·n**ee** _kahr_·toh
Can I have a receipt?	**Mohu dostat stvrzenku?** moh·hoo _dohs_·taht
	stvrzehn·koo
Thank you.	**Děkuji.** _dyeh_·koo·yih

Where to Eat

Can you	**Můžete mi doporučit…?** _moo_·zheh·teh mih
recommend…?	_doh_·poh·roo·chiht…
a restaurant	**restauraci** _rehs_·tow·rah·tsih
a bar	**bar** bahr
a café	**bufet** _boo_·feht
a fast-food place	**rychlé občerstvení** _rihkh_·l**eh** _ohp_·chehrs·tfeh·n**ee**
a cheap restaurant	**levná restaurace** lev·naah reh·stah·oo·rah·tse
an expensive	**drahá restaurace** drah·haa reh·stah·oo·rah·tse
restaurant	
a restaurant with	**restaurace s dobrým výhledem z okna**
a good view	reh·stah·oo·rah·tse z dob·reem vee·hleh·dehm z ok·nah
an authentic/	**autentická/málo turistická restaurace**
a non-touristy	ahootentitskaa/maa·loh too·ris·tits·kaa
restaurant	reh·stah·oo·rah·tse

Reservations & Preferences

I'd like to reserve	**Chtěl** m/**Chtěla** f **bych si objednat stůl…** khtyehl/
a table…	_khtyeh_·lah bihkh sih _ohb_·yehd·naht st**oo**hl…
for two	**pro dva** proh dvah
for this evening	**na dnes večer** _nah_·dnehs _veh_·chehr

for tomorrow at...	**na zítra na...**	_nah_·**zeet**·rah nah...
A table for two, please.	**Stůl pro dva, prosím.**	stoohl proh dvah _proh_·**seem**
We have a reservation.	**Máme tu rezervaci.**	_mah_·meh too _reh_·zehr·vah·tsih
I have a reservation.	**Mám rezervaci.**	Maahm reh·zehr·vah·tsih
My name is...	**Jmenuji se...**	_ymeh_·noo·yih seh...
Could we sit...?	**Mohli bychom si sednout...?**	_moh_·lih _bih_·khohm sih **sehd**·noht
here/there	**tady/tam**	_tah_·dih/tahm
outside	**venku**	_vehn_·koo
in a non-smoking area	**v části pro nekuřáky**	_fchahs_·tih proh neh·koo·rzh**ah**·kih
by the window	**u okna**	_oo_·ohk·nah
in the shade	**ve stínu**	veh styee·noo
in the sun	**na slunci**	nah sloon·tsy
Where are the restrooms [toilets]?	**Kde jsou záchody?**	gdeh ysoh _zah_·khoh·dih

---

YOU MAY HEAR...

Máte rezervaci? _mah_·teh _reh_·zehr·vah·tsih	Do you have a reservation?
Kolik osob? _koh_·lihk oh·sohp	How many people?
Pro kuřáky nebo nekuřáky? _proh_ koo·rzh**ah**·kih _neh_·boh neh·koo·rzh**ah**·kih	Smoking or non-smoking?
Chcete si objednat? _khtseh_·teh sih oh·byehd·naht	Are you ready to order?
Co byste si přáli? tsoh _bih_·styeh sih _przh**ah**_·lih	What would you like?
Doporučil bych... _doh_·poh·roo·chihl bihkh...	I recommend...
Dobrou chuť. _doh_·broh khoot'	Enjoy your meal.

YOU MAY SEE...

RESERVED	Rezervováno
RESTROOMS	WC/Toalety
NO SMOKING	Zákaz kouření/Kouření zakázáno

How to Order

Waiter/Waitress!	**Pane vrchní/Paní vrchní!** _pah_·neh vrkhn_ee_/_pah_·nee vrkhn_ee_
We're ready to order.	**Chtěli bychom si objednat.** _khtyeh_·lih _bih_·khohm sih _ohb_·yehd·naht
May I see the drink menu?	**Mohl** m/**Mohla** f **bych vidět nápojový lístek?** mohl/_moh_·hlah bihkh _vih_·dyeht _nah_·poh·yoh·vee _lees_·tehk
I'd like...	**Chtěl** m/**Chtěla** f **bych...** khtyehl/_khtyeh_·lah bikh...
a bottle of...	**láhev...** _lah_·hehf...
a carafe of...	**džbánek...** _dzhbah_·nehk...
a glass of...	**sklenici...** _skleh_·nih·tsih...
The menu, please.	**Jídelní lístek, prosím.** _yee_·dehl·nee _lees_·tehk _proh_·seem
Do you have...?	**Máte...?** _mah_·teh...
a menu in English	**jídelní lístek v angličtině** _yee_·dehl·nee _lees_·tehk _vahng_·lihch·tih·nyeh
a fixed-price menu	**polední menu** _poh_·lehd·nee _meh_·nih
a children's menu	**jídelníček pro děti** _yee_·dehl·nee·chehk proh _dyeh_·tih
What do you recommend?	**Co byste mi doporučil?** tsoh _bih_·steh mih _doh_·poh·roo·chihl
What's this?	**Co to je?** tsoh toh yeh
What's in it?	**Z čeho to je?** _scheh_·hoh toh yeh
Is it spicy?	**Je to pikantní?** yeh toh _pih_·kahnt·nee

I can't eat...	**Nemůžu jíst...** *Neh·moo·zhu yeast...*
rare	**málo propečený** *Maah·loh proh·peh·cheh·nee*
medium	**středně propečený** *strzed·nye proh·peh·cheh·nee*
well-done	**silně propečený** *sil·nye proh·peh·cheh·nee*
More...please.	**Více...prosím.** *vee·tseh...proh·seem*
And/or	**a/nebo** *ah/neh·boh*
I can't have...	**Nesmím jíst nic...** *nehs·meem yeest nihts...*
With/Without...	**S/Bez...** *s/behs...*
It's to go [take away].	**Vezmu si to s sebou.** *vehz·moo sih toh sseh·boh*

For Drinks, see page 73.

For Drinks, see page 73.

YOU MAY SEE...

JÍDELNÍ LÍSTEK	menu
NABÍDKA DNE	menu of the day
KUVERT A SERVIS (NENÍ) V CENĚ JÍDLA	cover charge and service (not) included in price
OBSLUHA NENÍ/JE ZAJIŠTĚNA	service (not) included
SPECIÁLNÍ PŘÍLOHY	specials

Cooking Methods

baked	**pečené** *peh·cheh·neh*
boiled	**vařené** *vah·rzheh·neh*
braised	**dušené** *doo·sheh·neh*
breaded	**ve strouhance** *veh·stroh·hahn·tseh*
creamed	**ve smetaně** *veh·smeh·tah·nyeh*
diced	**nakrájené na kostičky** *nah·krah·yeh·neh nah·kohs·tihch·kih*
fileted	**filé** *fih·leh*
fried	**smažené** *smah·zheh·neh*

grilled	**grilované** _grih·loh·vah·neh_
poached	**z vody** _sfoh·dih_
roasted	**pečené** _peh·cheh·neh_
sautéed	**na másle** _nah·mah·sleh_
smoked	**uzené** _oo·zheh·neh_
steamed	**dušené v páře** _doo·sheh·neh fpah·rzheh_
stewed	**dušené** _doo·sheh·neh_
stuffed	**plněné** _plnyeh·neh_

Dietary Requirements

I'm diabetic.	**Jsem diabetik.** _ysehm dyah·beh·tihk_
I'm lactose intolerant.	**Mám intoleranci laktózy.** _mahm ihn·toh·leh·rahn·tsih lahk·toh·zih_
I'm a vegetarian.	**Jsem vegetarián.** _ysehm veh·geh·tah·ryahn_
I'm vegan.	**Jsem vegán m/vegánka f.** _Sehm ve·ghaahn/ ve·ghaahn·kah_
I'm allergic to...	**Mám alergii na...** _mahm ah·lehr·gyih nah..._
I can't eat...	**Nesmím jíst nic...** _nehs·meem yeest nihts..._
dairy	**mléčné výrobky** _mlehch·neh vee·rohb·kih_
gluten	**gluten** _gloo·tehn_
nuts	**ořechy** _orzheh·khih_
pork	**vepřové** _vehp·rzoh·veh_
shellfish	**mořské plody** _mohrzhs·keh ploh·dih_
spicy foods	**pikantní jídla** _pih·kahnt·nee jeed·lah_
wheat	**pšeniční produkty** _psheh·nihch·nee proh·dook·tih_
Is it kosher?	**Je to košer/halal?** _yeh toh koh·shehr/hah·lahl_
Do you have...?	**Máte...?** _Maa·teh?_
skimmed milk	**polotučné mléko** _poh·loh·tooch·neh mleh·koh_
whole milk	**plnotučné mléko** _pl·noh·tooch·neh mleh·koh_
soya milk	**sójové mléko** _soh·yoh·veh mleh·koh_

Dining with Children

Do you have children's portions?	**Máte porce pro děti?** *mah·teh pohr·tseh proh dyeh·tih*
A highchair/child's seat, please.	**Židličku/Židli pro dítě, prosím.** *zhihd·lihch·koo/ zhihd·lih proh dee·tyeh proh·seem*
Where can I feed/ change the baby?	**Kde mohu nakojit/přebalit dítě?** *gdeh moh·hoo nah·koh·yiht/przheh·bah·liht dee·tyeh*
Can you warm this?	**Můžete mi to přihřát?** *mooh·zheh·teh mih toh przhih·hrzhaht*

For Traveling with Children, see page 148.

How to Complain

How much longer will our food be?	**Jak dlouho budeme ještě na jídlo čekat?** *yahk dloh·hoh boo·deh·meh yehsh·tyeh nah·yeed·loh cheh·kaht*
We can't wait any longer.	**Už nemůžeme déle čekat.** *oozh neh·moo·zheh·meh deh·leh cheh·kaht*
We're leaving.	**Odcházíme.** *oht·khah·zee·meh*
I didn't order this.	**To jsem si neobjednal m/neobjednala f.** *toh ysehm sih neh·ohb·yehd·nahl/neh·ohb·yehd·nah·lah*
I ordered…	**Objednal m/Objednala f jsem si…** *ohb·yehd·nahl/ ohb·yehd·nah·lah ysehm sih…*
I can't eat this.	**Nemohu to jíst.** *neh·moh·hoo toh yeest*
This is too…	**Tohle je moc…** *toh·hleh yeh mohts…*
cold/hot	**studené/horké** *stoo·deh·neh/hohr·keh*
salty/spicy	**slané/pikantní** *slah·neh/pih·kahnt·nee*
tough/bland	**tvrdé/mdlé** *tfrdeh/mdleh*
This isn't clean.	**Tohle není čisté.** *toh·hleh neh·nee chihs·teh*
This isn't fresh.	**Není to čerstvé.** *neh·nee toh chehrs·tfeh*

Paying

The check [bill], please.	**Účet, prosím.** _oo_-cheht _proh_-seem
We'd like to pay separately.	**Budeme platit každý samostatně.** _boo_-deh-meh _plah_-tiht _kazh_-dee _sah_-mohs-taht-nyeh
It's all together.	**Všechno dohromady.** _fshehkh_-noh _doh_-hroh-mah-di
Is service included?	**Je v tom zahrnutá obsluha?** yeh ftohm _zah_-hrnoo-**tah** _ohp_-sloo-hah
What's this amount for?	**Za co je tato částka?** _zah_-tsoh yeh _tah_-toh _chahst_-kal
I didn't have that. I had…	**To jsem neměl** _m_/**neměla** _f_. **Měl** _m_/**Měla** _f_ **jsem…** toh ysehm _neh_-myehl/_neh_-myeh-lah myehl/_myeh_-lah ysehm…
Can I pay by credit card?	**Mohu zaplatit kreditní kartou?** _moh_-hoo _zah_-plah-tiht _kreh_-diht-**nee** _kahr_-toh
Can I have an itemized bill/a receipt?	**Mohli byste mi účet rozepsát/dát stvrzenku?** _moh_-hlih _bihs_-teh mih **oo**-cheht roh-zehp-**saht**/daht _stvrzehn_-koo
That was a very good meal.	**Výborně jsem se najedl** _m_/**najedla** _f_. _vee_-bohr-nyel ysehm seh na-yehdl/nah-yehd-lah
That was delicious/ terrible.	**To bylo výborné/odporné** Toh bih-loh vee-bor-neh/od-pohr-neh
I've already paid.	**Už jsem zaplatil/zaplatila.** Uzh sem zah-plah-tyil

---

If a service charge is included in the price, you'll usually see **obsluha zahrnutá** (service included) written on the menu or on the bill. If the tip is not included, it's customary to leave 5-10%. Either hand the tip to your server and say **děkuji** (thank you) or **to je v pořádku** (it's OK), or simply leave the tip on the table.

Meals & Cooking

Breakfast

chléb *khlehb*	bread
džem *dzhehm*	jam
džus *dzhoos*	juice
jogurt *yoh-goort*	yogurt
káva *kah-vah*	coffee
kukuřičné vločky *koo-koo-rzhihch-neh vlohch-kih*	corn flakes
máslo *mah-sloh*	butter
med *meht*	honey
mléko *mleh-koh*	milk
topinka *toh-pihn-kah*	toast
...vejce ... *vehy-tseh*	...egg
míchaná *mee-khah-nah*	scrambled
smažená *smah-zheh-nah*	fried
vařená *vah-rzheh-nah*	boiled

Appetizers

křenová rolka *krzheh-noh-vah rohl-kah*	ham and horseradish roll
ruská vejce *roos-kah vehy-tseh*	egg with mayonnaise
salám s okurkou *sah-lahm soh-koor-koh*	salami with pickles
šunka s okurkou *shoon-kah soh-koor-koh*	ham with pickles

Traditional Czech cuisine can be rather heavy, with many meals centered around hearty soups and dumplings, roasted and fried meat (especially pork) and poultry, accompanied by dense sauces, and sides of potatoes and cabbage.

šunka v aspiku _shoon_·kah _vahs_·pih·koo	ham in aspic
tlačenka s cibulí _tlah_·chehn·kah _stsih_·boo·_lee_	rolled pork with onion
tresčí játra s cíbulkou _trehs_·chee _yah_·trah _stsee_·bool·koh	cod liver with onion
uzený jazyk _oo_·zeh·_nee yah_·zihk	smoked tongue
zavináče _zah_·vih·_nah_·cheh	pickled herring [rollmops]

Soup

bramboračka _brahm_·boh·rahch·kah	a thick soup with cubed potatoes, vegetables, mushrooms and garlic
bramborová polévka _brahm_·boh·roh·_vah_ poh·_lehf_·kah	potato soup
česneková polévka chehs·neh·koh·_vah_ poh·_lehf_·kah	garlic soup
čočková polévka _chohch_·koh·_vah_ poh·_lehf_·kah	lentil soup
fazolová polévka _fah_·zoh·loh·_vah_ poh·_lehf_·kah	bean soup
hovězí vývar (s nudlemi) _hoh_·vyeh·_zee vee_·vahr (snood·leh·mih)	consommé (with noodles)

hovězí vývar s játrovými noky *hoh*-vyeh-zee vee-vahr syah-troh-vee-mih noh-kih — beef broth and liver dumplings

hrachová polévka s uzeným *hrah*-khoh-vah poh-lehf-kah soo-zeh-neem — pea soup with smoked meat

kuřecí vývar (se zeleninou) *koo*-rzheh-tsee vee-vahr (seh-zeh-leh-nih-noh) — chicken soup (with vegetables)

rajská polévka *rahy*-skah poh-lehf-kah — tomato soup

rybí polévka *rih*-bee poh-lehf-kah — fish soup

zeleninová polévka *zeh*-leh-nih-noh-vah poh-lehf-kah — vegetable soup

zelná polévka *zehl*-nah poh-lehf-kah — cabbage soup

zelňačka *zehl*-n'ahch-kah — a thick soup with potatoes, sauerkraut and cream

Some of the best Czech **polévki** (soups) to be sampled include the traditional **hovězí vývar** (beef broth) with noodles and **česnekačka** (garlic soup with egg and small pieces of toasted bread). Other popular soups are **gulášová polévka** (goulash soup) and **dršťková polévka** (tripe soup), which is generously seasoned with sweet pepper.

Fish & Seafood

candát *tsahn*-daht — pike perch

garnát *gahr*-naht — shrimp [prawn]

humr *hoomr* — lobster

chobotnice *khoh*-boht-nih-tseh — octopus

kapr... *kahpr...* — carp...

   smažený *smah*-zheh-nee — fried in bread crumbs

na černo _nah_·chehr·noh — in a thick sauce of vegetables, dark beer and prunes

na česneku _nah_·chehs·neh·koo — grilled with butter and garlic

kaviár _kah_·vy**ahr** — caviar

krab _krahb_ — crab

losos _loh_·sohs — salmon

mořský jazyk _mohrzh_·sk**ee** _yah_·zihk — sole

platýz _plah_·t**ees** — plaice

pstruh na másle _pstrooh_ nah _mah_·sleh — trout fried in butter

rybí filé _rih_·bee _fih_·leh — fish fillet

slaneček _slah_·neh·chehk — herring

štika _shtih_·kah — pike

treska _trehs_·kah — cod

tuňák _too_·n'ahk — tuna

ústřice _oo_·strzhih·tseh — oyster

Meat & Poultry

bažant _bah_·zhahnt — pheasant

biftek _bihf_·tehk — steak

guláš _goo_·lahsh — goulash

hovězí _hoh_·vyeh·zee — beef

husa _hoo_·sah — goose

jehněčí _yeh_·hnyeh·chee — lamb

kachna _kahkh_·nah — duck

klobása _kloh_·bah·sah — sausage

králík _krah_·leek — rabbit

krůta _krooh_·tah — turkey

kuře _koo_·rzheh — chicken

párka _pahr_·kah — type of thick sausage

slanina _slah_·nih·nah — bacon

One of the best-known Czech dishes is **vepřo-knedlo-zelo** (pork with fried cabbage) and **knedlíky** (dumplings). There are two types of **knedlíky**: **houskové knedlíky** (made of flour) and **bramborové knedlíky** (made with potatoes). The latter are usually served with duck or goose together with red cabbage boiled in red wine. The highlight of Czech cuisine is **svíčková na smetaně** (beef fillet in a cream and vegetable sauce), served, naturally, with **knedlíky**.

šunka _shoon•kah_	ham
telecí _teh•leh•tsee_	veal
vepřové _vehp•rzhoh•veh_	pork
zajíc _zah•yeets_	hare
zvěřina _zvyeh•rzhih•nah_	game

Vegetables

brambor _brahm•bohr_	potato
celer _tseh•lehr_	celery
cibule _tsih•boo•leh_	onion
cuketa _tsoo•keh•tah_	zucchini [courgette]
červená řepa _chehr•veh•nah rzheh•pah_	beet [beetroot]
česnek _chehs•nehk_	garlic
fazolové lusky _fah•zoh•loh•veh loos•kih_	green beans
houba _hoh•bah_	mushroom
hrášek _hrah•shehk_	peas
jarní cibulka _yahr•nee tsih•bool•kah_	spring onion
květák _kvyeh•tahk_	cauliflower
lilek _lih•lehk_	eggplant [aubergine]
mrkev _mrkehf_	carrot

okurka <u>oh</u>·koor·kah	cucumber
paprika <u>pahp</u>·rih·kah	pepper
pórek <u>poh</u>·rehk	leek
rajče <u>rahy</u>·cheh	tomato
salát <u>sah</u>·laht	lettuce
šalotka <u>shah</u>·loht·kah	shallot
zelí <u>zeh</u>·lee	cabbage
žampiony <u>zhahm</u>·pyoh·nih	mushrooms

Fruit

banán <u>bah</u>·nahn	banana
borůvka <u>boh</u>·roof·kah	blueberry
broskev <u>brohs</u>·kehv	peach
grep grehp	grapefruit
hrozno <u>hrohz</u>·noh	grape
jablko <u>yah</u>·blkoh	apple
jahoda <u>yah</u>·hoh·dah	strawberry
malina <u>mah</u>·lih·nah	raspberry
meloun <u>meh</u>·lohn	melon
meruňka <u>meh</u>·roon'·kah	apricot
pomeranč <u>poh</u>·meh·rahnch	orange
švestka <u>shfehst</u>·kah	plum
třešeň <u>trzheh</u>·shehn'	cherry
višeň <u>vih</u>·shehn'	sour cherry
vodní meloun vohd·nee <u>meh</u>·lohn	watermelon

Cheese

jemný sýr <u>yehm</u>·nee seer	mild cheese
kozí sýr <u>koh</u>·zee seer	goat cheese
měkký tvaroh <u>myehk</u>·kee <u>tfah</u>·rohh	cottage cheese
Niva® <u>nih</u>·vah	common brand of blue cheese available

ostrý sýr <u>ohs</u>•tree seer	pungent cheese
ovčí sýr <u>ohf</u>•chee seer	ewe's milk cheese
plísňový sýr <u>plees</u>•ňoh•vee seer	blue cheese
smažený sýr <u>sma</u>•zhe•nee seer	cheese fried in bread crumbs
smetanový sýr <u>smeh</u>•tah•noh•vee seer	cream cheese
syrečky <u>sih</u>•rehch•kih	pungent cheese made with beer
tvrdý sýr tfrdee seer	hard cheese

Dessert

jablečný závin <u>yahb</u>•lehch•nee <u>zah</u>•vihn	apple strudel
kobliha <u>kohb</u>•lih•hah	donut
lívance <u>lee</u>•vahn•tseh	small pancakes, spread with plums and a layer of cottage cheese, topped with yogurt or thick sour cream
makový koláč <u>mah</u>•koh•vee <u>koh</u>•lahch	poppy seed cake
medovník <u>meh</u>•dohv•neek	honey cake
ovocný koláč <u>oh</u>•vohts•nee <u>koh</u>•lahch	fruit cake
ovocný koláč s drobenkou <u>oh</u>•vohts•nee <u>koh</u>•lahch <u>sdroh</u>•behn•koh	fruit crumble pie

palačinka _pah·lah·chihn·kah_   thin pancake
švestkové knedlíky _shvehst·koh·veh_   plum dumplings sprinkled
knehd·lee·kih   with curd cheese and sugar
                                                      and covered with melted
                                                      butter

trubičky se šlehačkou _troo·bihch·kih_   brandy cake rolls with
seh·shleh·hahch·koh   cream
tvarohové taštičky _tfah·roh·hoh·veh_   cottage cheese pastries
tash·tihch·kih
zmrzlina _zmrzlih·nah_   ice cream

Sauces & Condiments

hořčice _horz·chi·tse_   mustard
kečup _keh·tshoop_   ketchup
pepř _pehprzh_   pepper
sůl _sool_   salt

At the Market

Where are the carts [trolleys]/baskets?	**Kde jsou vozíky/košíky?** _gdeh ysoh voh·zee·kih/ koh·shee·kih_
Where is...?	**Kde je...?** _gdeh yeh..._
I'd like some of that/ those.	**Chtěl** _m_/**Chtěla** _f_ **bych to/tamto.** _khtyehl/khtyeh·lah bihkh toh/tahm·toh_
Can I taste it?	**Můžu to ochutnat?** _moo·zhoo toh oh·khoot·naht_

YOU MAY SEE...

KALORIE	calories
BEZ TUKU	fat free
USCHOVEJTE V CHLADU	keep refrigerated
PRODAT PŘED...	sell by...
HODIT SE PRO VEGETARIANY	suitable for vegetarians

YOU MAY HEAR...

Čím posloužím? *cheem pohs•loh•zheem*   Can I help you?
Co si přejete? *tsoh sih przheh•yeh•teh*   What would you like?
Ještě něco? *yehsh•tyeh nyeh•tsoh*   Anything else?
...korun. *. . .koh•roon*   That's...crowns.

I'd like...	**Chtěl** *m*/**Chtěla** *f* **bych...** *khtyehl/khtyeh•lah bihkh...*	
a kilo/ half-kilo of...	**kilo/půl kila...** *kih•loh/pool kih•lah...*	
a liter/ half-liter of...	**litr/půl litru...** *lihtr/pool liht•roo...*	
a piece of...	**kousek...** *koh•sehk...*	
a slice of...	**pláteček...** *plah•teh•chehk...*	
More/Less.	**Trošku více/méně.** *trohsh•koo vih•tseh/meh•nyeh*	
How much?	**Kolik?** *koh•lihk*	
Where do I pay?	**Kde zaplatím?** *gdeh zah•plah•teem*	
A bag, please.	**Tašku, prosím.** *tahsh•koo proh•seem*	
I'm being helped.	**Už mne obsluhují.** *oosh mneh ohp•sloo•hoo•yee*	

For Conversion Tables, see page 180.

Measurements in Europe are metric - and that applies to the weight of food too. If you tend to think in pounds and ounces, it's worth brushing up on what the metric equivalent is before you go shopping for fruit and veg in markets and supermarkets. Five hundred grams, or half a kilo, is a common quantity to order, and that converts to just over a pound (17.65 ounces, to be precise).

In the Kitchen

bottle opener	**otvírač na láhve**	_oht_•**fee**•rahch _nah_•**lah**•hfeh
bowl	**miska**	_mihs_•kah
can opener	**otvírač na plechovky**	_oht_•**fee**•rach _nah_•pleh•khohf•kih
corkscrew	**vývrtka**	_vee_•vrtkah
cup	**šálek**	_shah_•lehk
fork	**vidlička**	_vih_•dlihch•kah
frying pan	**pánev**	_pah_•nehf
glass	**sklenice**	_skleh_•nih•tseh
knife	**nůž**	_noo_zh
measuring cup/spoon	**odměrka/měření lžice**	_ohd_•myehr•kah/ _myeh_•rzheh•**nee** _lzhih_•tseh
napkin	**ubrousek**	_oob_•roh•sehk
plate	**talíř**	_tah_•**lee**rzh
pot	**konvice**	_kohn_•vih•tseh
saucepan	**hrnec**	hrnehts
spatula	**lopatka**	_loh_•paht•kah
spoon	**lžíce**	_lzhee_•tseh

ESSENTIAL

May I see the wine list/drink menu, please?	**Smím prosit vínný lístek/nápojový lístek?** _smeem <u>proh</u>•siht veen•nee <u>lees</u>•tehk/ nah•poh•yoh•vee <u>lees</u>•tehk_
What do you recommend?	**Co mi můžete doporoučit?** _tsoh mih <u>moo</u>•zheh•teh doh•poh•roh•chiht_
I'd like a bottle/glass of red/white wine.	**Chtěl m/Chtěla f bych láhev/pohár červeného/ bílého vína.** _khtyehl/<u>khteh</u>•lah bihkh <u>lah</u>•hef/ poh•hahr <u>chehr</u>•veh•neh•hoh/<u>bee</u>•leh•hoh <u>vee</u>•nah_
The house wine, please.	**Stolní víno, prosím.** _<u>stohl</u>•nee <u>vee</u>•noh <u>proh</u>•seem_
Another bottle/ glass, please.	**Ještě jednu láhev/pohár, prosím.** _yeh•shtyeh yehd•noo <u>lah</u>•hehf/poh•hahr <u>proh</u>•seem_
I'd like a local beer.	**Chtěl m/Chtěla f bych místní pivo.** _khtyehl/ <u>khtyeh</u>•lah bihkh <u>meest</u>•nee pih•voh_
Can I buy you a drink?	**Mohu vám objednat něco k pití?** _<u>moh</u>•hoo vahm ohb•yehd•naht nyeh•tsoh kpih•tee_
Cheers!	**Na zdraví!** _<u>nah</u>•zdrah•vee_
A coffee/tea, please.	**Kávu/Čaj, prosím.** _<u>kah</u>•voo/chahy <u>proh</u>•seem_
A ..., please.	**...prosím.** _.... <u>proh</u>•seem_
juice	**Džus** _dzhoos_
soda	**Sodou** _soh•doh_
(sparkling/still) water	**Vodu (s bublinkami/bez bublinek)** _<u>voh</u>•doo (zboob•lihn•kah•mih/<u>behz</u>•boob•lih•nehk)_
Is the tap water safe to drink?	**Může se pít kohoutková voda?** _<u>moo</u>•zheh seh peet koh•hoht•koh•vah <u>voh</u>•dah_

YOU MAY HEAR...

Mohu vám objednat něco k pití? moh·hoo vahm ohb·yehd·naht nyeh·tsoh kpih·tee   Can I get you a drink?

Bílou/S cukrem? bee·loh/stsook·rehm   With milk/sugar?

Voda s bublinkami nebo bez bublinek? voh·dah zboob·lihn·kah·mih neh·boh behz boob·lih·nehk   Sparkling or still water?

Non-alcoholic Drinks

čaj chahy	tea
...džus ...dzhoos	...juice
jablečný yahb·lehch·nee	apple
pomerančový poh·meh·rahn·choh·vee	orange
rajský rahy·skee	tomato
horkou čokoládu hohr·koh choh·koh·lah·doo	hot chocolate
(bílou/černou) kávu (bee·loh/chehr·noh) kah·voo	coffee (with milk/black)
kávu s cukrem/umělým sladidlem kah·voo s tsook·rehm/oo·myeh·leem slah·dih·dlehm	coffee with sugar/artificial sweetener
kávu bez kofeinu kah·voo behs koh·feh·yih·noo	decaffeinated coffee
kolu koh·loo	cola
limonádu lih·moh·nah·doo	lemonade
mléko mleh·koh	milk
mléčný koktejl mleh·chnee kohk·tehyl	milk shake
minerálku (s bublinkami/bez bublinek) mih·neh·rahl·koo (zboob·lihn·kah·mih/behz boob·lih·nehk)	(sparkling/still) mineral water

Among hot drinks, the most popular is **káva** (coffee), enjoyed throughout the whole day. Prague is home to many popular **kavárny** (coffee houses); these are excellent places to enjoy local life. As to **čaj** (tea), Czechs often joke that it is a drink for kids, while adults drink it only in winter (and even then with rum).

Among cold drinks, a typically Czech beverage is **Kofola®** (a cola that includes fruit extracts), which can be bought in bottles or cans, and also from the barrel as **čepovaná kofola**. Mineral water is also readily available; well-known brands include: **Aquila®**, **Dobrá Voda®**, **Hanácka Kyselka®**, **Karlovarské®**, **Poděbradka®**, **Rajec®** and **Toma Voda®**.

Aperitifs, Cocktails & Liqueurs

anýzovka *ah·nee·zohf·kah*	aniseed liqueur
brandy *brehn·dih*	brandy
džin *dzhihn*	gin
džin fiz *dzhihn fihz*	gin fizz
džin s tonikem *dzhihn stoh·nih·kehm*	gin and tonic
meruňkovice *meh·roon'·koh·vih·tseh*	apricot brandy
pálenka *pah·lehn·kah*	brandy
slivovice *slih·voh·vih·tseh*	plum brandy
šery *sheh·rih*	sherry
vodka *voht·kah*	vodka
vermut *vehr·moot*	vermouth
whisky *vihs·kih*	whisky

The turning point for Czech brewing was October 5, 1842, when the technology of bottom fermentation was used for the first time and **světlý ležák** (pale lager) **Pilsner Urquell**® was produced. Apart from **Pilsner Urquell**® (called simply **Plzeň** by Czechs), other popular Czech beer brands are: **Budějovický Budvar**®, **Velkopopovický Kozel**®, **Radegast**®, **Staropramen**® and **Gambrinus**®. In addition to these, one may also order **řezane**: dark and light beer poured into one glass in such a way that it creates two distinct layers.

Beer

černé _chehr_·neh		stout
láhvové _lah_·hfoh·veh		bottled
ležák _leh_·zhahk		lager
místní pivo _meest_·nee _pih_·voh		local beer
pivo _pih_·voh		beer
plzeňské _plzehn'_·skeh		pilsner
pšeničné pivo _psheh_·nih·chneh _pih_·voh		wheat beer
světlé _svyeht_·leh		light
točené _toh_·cheh·neh		draft [draught]

Wine

...víno ... _vee_·noh		...wine
bílé _bee_·leh		white
červené _chehr_·veh·neh		red
růžové _roo_·zhoh·veh		blush [rosé]
sladké _slaht_·keh		sweet
suché _soo_·kheh		dry
šumivé _shoo_·mih·veh		sparkling

alkoholický nápoj _ahl·koh·hoh·lihts·kee_
nah·pohy — alcoholic drink

ananas _ah·nah·nahs_ — pineapple

angrešt _ahn·gresht_ — gooseberry

anýz _ah·neez_ — aniseed

anýzovka _ah·nee·zohf·kah_ — aniseed liqueur

aperitiv _ah·peh·rih·tihf_ — aperitif

arašíd _ah·rah·sheed_ — peanut

artyčok _ahr·tih·chohk_ — artichoke

aspik _ahs·pihk_ — jelly

avokádo _ah·voh·kah·doh_ — avocado

banán _bah·nahn_ — banana

banán v čokoládí — chocolate-covered banana
bah·nahn fchoh·koh·lah·dee

bazalka _bah·zahl·kah_ — basil

bažant _bah·zhahnt_ — pheasant

bez kofeinu _behs·koh·feh·yih·noo_ — decaffeinated

biftek _bihf·tehk_ — steak

bílé hrozen _bee·leh hroh·zehn_ — green grape

bílé zelí _bee·leh zeh·lee_ — white cabbage

bílek _bee·lehk_ — egg white

bílý chléb _bee·lee khlehb_ — white bread

bob _bohb_ — broad bean

bobkový list _bohb·koh·vee lihst_ — bay leaf

bonbón _bohn·bohn_ — candy [sweet]

borůvka _boh·roof·kah_ — blueberry

borůvkový knedlík _boh·roof·koh·vee_ — blueberry dumpling
knehd·leek

borůvkový koláč _boh·roof·koh·vee koh·lahch_ — blueberry pie

brambor _brahm_•bohr	potato
bramboračka _brahm_•boh•rahch•kah	thick soup with potatoes and vegetables
bramborák _brahm_•boh•**rahk**	potato pancake
bramborová kaše _brahm_•boh•roh•**vah** kah•sheh	mashed potato
bramborová polévka _brahm_•boh•roh•**vah** poh•**lehf**•kah	potato soup
bramborové hranolky _brahm_•boh•roh•**veh** hrah•nohl•kih	French fries
bramborové taštičky s masitou nádivkou _brahm_•boh•roh•**veh** tahsh•tihch•kih _smah_•sih•toh **nah**•dihf•koh	potato ravioli with meat filling
bramborový knedlík _brahm_•boh•roh•**vee** knehd•**leek**	potato dumpling
bramborový kroket _brahm_•boh•roh•**vee** kroh•keht	potato croquette
brokolice _broh_•koh•lih•tseh	broccoli
broskev _brohs_•kehf	peach
brusinka _broo_•sihn•kah	cranberry
bůček _boo_•chehk	brisket

buchta _boo_·khtah	sweet bun
burský oříšek _boor_·skee oh·rzhee·shehk	peanut
bylinka _bih_·lihn·kah	herb
bylinková směs _bih_·lihn·koh·vah smyehs	mixed herbs
candát _tsahn_·daht	pike perch
celer _tseh_·lehr	celery
celozrnná mouka _tseh_·lohz·rnah moh·kah	whole-wheat flour
cemr _tsehmr_	loin
chléb _khlehb_	bread
cibule _tsih_·boo·leh	onion
citrón _tsih_·trohn	lemon
citrónový džus _tsiht_·roh·noh·vee dzhoos	lemon juice
cuketa _tsoo_·keh·tah	zucchini [courgette]
cukr _tsookr_	sugar
cukrová kukuřice _tsook_·roh·vah koo·koo·rzhih·tseh	corn [sweet corn]
cukroví _tsook_·roh·vee	small sweet pastries
čaj _chahy_	tea
čekanka _cheh_·kahn·kah	chicory
černou _chehr_·noh	black (coffee)
černý rybíz _chehr_·nee rih·bees	black currant
čerstvý _chehrs_·tfee	fresh
čerstvý ovoc _chehrs_·tfee oh·vohts	fresh fruit
čerstvý tvaroh _chehrs_·tfee tfah·roh	fresh curd cheese
červená řepa _chehr_·veh·nah rzheh·pah	beet [beetroot]
červené zelí _chehr_·veh·neh zeh·lee	red cabbage
červený _chehr_·veh·nee	red (wine)
červený hrozen _chehr_·veh·nee hroh·zehn	red grape
červený rybíz _chehr_·veh·nee rih·bees	red currant
česnek _chehs_·nehk	garlic
česneková majonéza _chehs_·neh·koh·vah	garlic mayonnaise

mah•yoh•neh•zah

česneková omáčka *chehs•neh•koh•vah oh•mah•chkah* — garlic sauce

česneková polévka *chehs•neh•koh•vah poh•lehf•kah* — garlic soup

čevapčiči *cheh•vahp•chih•chih* — meatballs

čínské zelí *cheen•skeh zeh•lee* — Chinese cabbage

čistý *chihs•tee* — straight [neat]

čočka *chohch•kah* — lentil

čočková polévka *chohch•koh•vah poh•lehf•kah* — lentil soup

čočkový salát *chohch•koh•vee sah•laht* — lentil salad

čokoláda *choh•koh•lah•dah* — chocolate

chlazený *khlah•zeh•nee* — chilled, iced (drink)

chlazený nápoj *khlah•zeh•nee nah•pohy* — cold drink

chléb *khlehb* — bread

chlebíček *khleh•bee•chehk* — open sandwich

chlupatý knedlík *khloo•pah•tee knehd•leek* — dumpling with diced, smoke← meat and sauerkraut

chobotnice *khoh•boht•nih•tseh* — octopus

chřest *khrzhehst* — asparagus

chuťovky *khoo•t'ohf•kih* — spicy appetizers [starters]

cukr *tsookr* — sugar

datle *daht•leh* — date

dezert *deh•zehrt* — dessert

dezertní víno *deh•zehrt•nee vee•noh* — dessert wine

divočák *dih•voh•chahk* — wild boar

domácí *doh•mah•tsee* — homemade

dort *dohrt* — cake

dršťková polévka *drsht'koh•vah poh•lehf•kah* — tripe soup

dršťky *drsht'kih* — tripe

drůbež <u>droo</u>•behzh	poultry
drůbky <u>droob</u>•kih	giblets
dušená ryba <u>doo</u>•sheh•nah <u>rih</u>•bah	steamed fish
dušená rýže <u>doo</u>•sheh•nah **ree**•zheh	steamed rice
dušené ovoce <u>doo</u>•sheh•neh <u>oh</u>•voh•tseh	stewed fruit
dušené telecí maso na víně <u>doo</u>•sheh•**neh** teh•leh•ts**ee** mah•soh nah•**vee**•nyeh	veal braised in wine
dýně <u>dee</u>•nyeh	pumpkin
džem dzhehm	jam
džin dzhihn	gin
džin s tonikem dzhihn <u>stoh</u>•nih•kehm	gin and tonic
džus dzhoos	juice
estragon <u>ehs</u>•trah•gohn	tarragon
fazole <u>fah</u>•zoh•leh	beans
fazolová polévka <u>fah</u>•zoh•loh•**vah** poh•**lehf**•kah	bean soup
fazolové klíčky <u>fah</u>•zoh•loh•**veh** <u>kleech</u>•kih	bean sprouts
fenykl <u>feh</u>•nihkl	fennel
fík feek	fig
francouzská zálivka <u>frahn</u>•tsohs•**kah** <u>zah</u>•lihf•kah	vinaigrette [French dressing]

granát _grah_·naht	shrimp [prawn]
granátové jablko _grah_·nah·toh·v**eh** _yahbl_·koh	pomegranate
gratinovaný _grah_·tih·noh·vah·n**ee**	au gratin
grep _grehp_	grapefruit
gril _grihl_	grill
grilované kuře _grih_·loh·vah·n**eh** _koo_·rzheh	grilled chicken
grilovaný na dřevěném uhlí _grih_·loh·vah·n**ee** _nah_·drzheh·vyeh·n**eh**m _oo_·hl**ee**	charcoal-grilled
guláš _goo_·lahsh	goulash (stew)
gulášová polévka _goo_·lah·shoh·v**ah** poh·**lehf**·kah	goulash soup
heřmánkový čaj _hehrzh_·**m**ahn·koh·v**ee** _chahy_	chamomile tea
hlavní jídla _hlahv_·n**ee** _yeed_·lah	entrées
hodně kořeněný _hohd_·nyeh _koh_·rzheh·nyeh·n**ee**	highly seasoned
holoub _hoh_·lohb	pigeon
horká voda _hohr_·kah _voh_·dah	hot water
horkou čokoládu _hohr_·koh _choh_·koh·**lah**·doo	hot chocolate

horký _hohr·kee_ — hot (temperature)

hořčice _hohrzh·chih·tseh_ — mustard

houba _hoh·bah_ — mushroom

houska _hohs·kah_ — roll

houskový knedlík _hohs·koh·vee knehd·leek_ — bread dumpling

hovězí _hoh·vyeh·zee_ — beef

hovězí pečeně _hoh·vyeh·zee peh·cheh·nyeh_ — roast beef

hovězí tokáň _hoh·vyeh·zee toh·kahn'_ — beef in wine and tomato purée

hovězí vývar _hoh·vyeh·zee vee·vahr_ — beef broth

hovězí vývar s játrovými knedlíčky _hoh·vyeh·zee vee·vahr syah·troh·vee·mih knehd·leech·kih_ — beef broth with liver dumplings

hrachor _hrah·khohr_ — sweet peas [mangetout]

hrachová polévka s uzeným masem _hrah·khoh·vah poh·lehf·kah soo·zeh·neem mah·sehm_ — pea soup with smoked meat

hranolky _hrah·nohl·kih_ — French fries

hrášek _hrah·shehk_ — peas

hrozinka _hroh·zihn·kah_ — raisin

hruška _hruh·shkah_ — pear

hřebíček _hrzheh·bee·chehk_ — clove

humr _hoomr_ — lobster

husa _hoo·sah_ — goose

jablečný džus _yahb·lehch·nee dzhoos_ — apple juice

jablečný závin _yahb·lehch·nee zah·vihn_ — apple strudel

jablko _yahbl·koh_ — apple

jablkový koláč _yahbl·koh·vee koh·lahch_ — apple pie

jahoda _yah·hoh·dah_ — strawberry

jarní cibulka _yahr·nee tsih·bool·kah_ — spring onion

játra _yah·trah_ — liver

játrová paštika _yah·troh·vah_ _pahsh·tih·kah_		liver paté
játrové knedlíčky _yah·troh·veh_ _kneh·dleech·kih_		liver balls (served in broth)
jazyk _yah·zihk_		tongue
jehněčí _yeh·hnyeh·chee_		lamb
jehněčí guláš _yeh·hnyeh·chee goo·lahsh_		lamb stew
jehněčí kýta _yeh·hnyeh·chee kee·tah_		leg of lamb
jelení _yeh·leh·nee_		venison
jelínek _yeh·lee·nehk_		brandy
jelito _yeh·lih·toh_		black pudding
jemný _yehm·nee_		mild (flavor)
jídelní lístek _yee·dehl·nee lees·tehk_		menu
jídlo _yeed·loh_		dish (meal)
jitrnice _yiht·rnih·tseh_		white sausage
jogurt _yoh·goort_		yogurt
kachna _kahkh·nah_		duck
kakao _kah·kah·oh_		cocoa
kandované ovoce _kahn·doh·vah·neh_ _oh·voh·tseh_		candied fruit
kapar _kah·pahr_		caper
kapoun _kah·pohn_		capon
kapr _kahpr_		carp
kapr na černo _kahpr nah·chehr·noh_		baked carp in beer, prune and vegetable sauce
kapr na česneku _kahpr nah·chehs·neh·koo_		carp grilled with butter and garlic
kapr na kmíně _kapr nah·kmee·nyeh_		carp baked with caraway seeds
kapustová polévka _kah·poos·toh·vah_ _poh·lehf·kah_		cabbage soup
karafa _kah·rah·fah_		carafe

karamel _kah_·rah·mehl — caramel

Karlovarská Becherovka® _kahr_·loh·vahrs·kah — bitter herb liqueur
beh·kheh·rohf·kah

kaštan _kah_·shtahn — chestnut

káva _kah_·vah — coffee

kaviár _kah_·vy**ah**r — caviar

kečup _keh_·choop — ketchup

kiwi _kee_·vee — kiwi fruit

klobáska _kloh_·b**ah**s·kah — sausage made with coarsely
ground pork

kmín km**ee**n — caraway

knedlík _knehd_·l**ee**k — dumpling

knedlík s vejci _knehd_·l**ee**k _sfehy_·tsih — dumpling with scrambled
eggs

kobliha _kohb_·lih·hah — donut

kokos _koh_·kohs — coconut

koláč _koh_·l**ah**ch — pie (sweet or savory)

koláček _koh_·l**ah**·chehk — tartlette (sweet or
savory)

kompot _kohm_·poht — stewed fruit

konsomé _kohn_·soh·m**eh** — consommé

kopr kohpr — dill

koroptev _koh_·rohp·tehf — partridge

kořeněný _koh_·rzheh·nyeh·n**ee** — hot, spicy, seasoned

koření _koh_·rzheh·n**ee** — seasoning, spices

kost kohst — bone

kotleta _koht_·leh·tah — chop

koza _koh_·zah — goat

kozí sýr _koh_·z**ee** s**ee**r — goat cheese

krab krahb — crab

krájený _krah_·yeh·n**ee** — sliced

králík _krah_·leek	rabbit
králík na smetaně _krah_·leek _nah_· smeh·tah·nyeh	roast rabbit in rich cream sauce
krekry _krehk_·rih	crackers
krémovitá polévka _kreh_·moh·vih·tah poh·_lehf_·kah	cream soup
kroketa _kroh_·keh·tah	croquette
kroupy _kroh_·pih	barley
krůta _kroo_·tah	turkey
křen krzhehn	horseradish
křepelka _krzheh_·pehl·kah	quail
kukuřice _koo_·koo·rzhih·tseh	corn
kuře _kooh_·rzheh	chicken
kuře na paprice _koo_·rzheh _nah_·pahp·rih·tseh	pan-roasted chicken with creamy paprika sauce
kuře pečené s nádivkou _koo_·rzheh peh·cheh·neh _snah_·dihf·koh	roast chicken with stuffing
kuřecí játra _koo_·rzheh·tsee _yaht_·rah	chicken liver
kuřecí prso _koo_·rzheh·tsee prsoh	breast of chicken
kuřecí vývar _koo_·rzheh·tsee _vee_·vahr	chicken broth
květák _kfyeh_·tahk	cauliflower
kyselé okurky _kih_·seh·leh oh·koor·kih	sour pickles
kyselé zelí _kih_·seh·leh _zeh_·lee	sauerkraut
kýta _kee_·tah	leg (cut of meat)
langoš _lahn_·gohsh	fried dough coated in garlic
led _lehd_	ice
ledvinky _lehd_·vih·kih	kidneys
lehký _lehh_·kee	light (sauce, etc.)
ležák _leh_·zhahk	lager
lihovina _lih_·hoh·vih·nah	spirits
likér _lih_·kehr	liqueur

lilek _lih_•lehk	eggplant [aubergine]
limetta _lih_•meht•tah	lime
limettový džus _lih_•meht•toh•**vee** dzhoos	lime juice
limonáda _lih_•moh•**nah**•dah	lemonade
lískový ořech _lees_•koh•vee oh•rzhehkh	hazelnut
lístkové těsto _leest_•koh•**veh** tyehs•toh	puff pastry
lišky _lihsh_•kih	chanterelle mushrooms
lívance _lee_•vahn•tseh	small pancakes with plum and cottage cheese, topped with yogurt or sour cream
lívanečky _lee_•vah•nehch•kih	fritters
losos _loh_•sohs	salmon
majonéza _mahy_•neh•zah	mayonnaise
majoránka _mah_•yoh•**rahn**•kah	marjoram
mák _mahk_	poppy seeds
makový koláč _mah_•koh•vee koh•**lahch**	poppy seed cake
makrela _mahk_•reh•lah	mackerel
malé občerstvení _mah_•**leh** _ohb_•chehr•stfeh•**nee**	snacks
malina _mah_•lih•nah	raspberry
mandarínka _mahn_•dah•**reen**•kah	tangerine
mandle _mahn_•dleh	almond
marcipán _mahr_•tsih•**pahn**	marzipan
marinovaný (v octě) _mah_•rih•noh•vah•**nee** (_fots_•tyeh)	marinated (in vinegar)
marmeládu _mahr_•meh•lah•doo	jam
máslo _mahs_•loh	butter
maso _mah_•soh	meat
masová směs na roštu _mah_•soh•**vah** smyehs _nah_•rohsh•too	mixed grill
masový a zeleninový vývar _mah_•soh•**vee**	meat and vegetable broth

ah zeh·leh·nih·noh·vee vee·vahr

máta *mah·tah* — mint

mečoun *meh·chohn* — swordfish

med *meht* — honey

medovnik *meh·doh·vnihk* — honey cake

melasa *meh·lah·sah* — molasses [treacle]

meloun *meh·lohn* — melon

meruňka *meh·roon'·kah* — apricot

meruňkovice *meh·roon'·koh·vih·tseh* — apricot brandy

meruňkový knedlík *meh·roon'·koh·vee knehd·leek* — apricot dumpling

míchaná zelenina *mee·khah·nah zeh·leh·nih·nah* — mixed vegetables

míchaný salát *mee·khah·nee sah·laht* — mixed salad

minerálka/minerální voda *mih·neh·rahl·kah/mih·neh·rahl·nih voh·dah* — mineral water

místní speciality *mees·tnee speh·tsyah·lih·tih* — local specialties

mléčný koktejl *mlehch·nee kohk·tehyl* — milk shake

mléko *mleh·koh* — milk

mleté maso _mleh•**teh** mah•soh_	ground meat [mince]
moravský vrabec _moh•rahfs•kee **vrah**•behts_	stewed slice of pork stuffed with ham, egg and pickle
moruše _moh•roo•sheh_	mulberry
mořský jazyk _mohrzh•skee **yah**•zihk_	sole
moučník _mohch•neek_	dessert
mouka _moh•kah_	flour
mozeček _moh•zeh•chehk_	brains
mrkev _mrkehf_	carrot
muškátový oříšek _moosh•**kah**•toh•vee oh•rzh**ee**•shehk_	nutmeg
na česneku _nah•chehs•neh•koo_	in garlic
na grilu _nah•grih•loo_	grilled
na kosti _nah•kohs•tih_	on the bone
na másle _nah•**mah**•sleh_	sautéed
na oleji _nah•oh•leh•yih_	in oil
na roštu _nah•rohsh•too_	barbecued
na rožni _nah•rohzh•nih_	spit-roasted
na špízu _nah•shp**ee**•zoo_	skewered
nadívané olivy _nah•dee•vah•neh oh•lih•vih_	stuffed olives
nádivka _**nah**•dihf•kah_	stuffing
nakládaná okurka _nah•k**lah**•dah•nah oh•koor•kah_	pickle
nakládané houby _nah•k**lah**•dah•neh hoh•bih_	pickled mushrooms
nakládaný _nah•k**lah**•dah•nee_	marinated
nakrájený na plátky _nah•krah•yeh•nee nah•p**lah**t•kih_	sliced
nakyselo _nah•kih•seh•loh_	sour (taste)
naměkko _nah•myehk•koh_	soft-boiled (eggs)
nápojový lístek _**nah**•poh•yoh•vee **lees**•tehk_	wine list

naťový celer *nah·t'oh·vee tseh·lehr*	celery
natvrdo *nah·tfrdoh*	hard-boiled (eggs)
nealkoholické nápoje *neh·ahl·koh·hoh·lihts·keh nah·poh·yeh*	non-alcoholic drinks
nektarinka *nehk·tah·rihn·kah*	nectarine
Niva® *nih·vah*	brand of blue cheese
nudle *nood·leh*	noodles
nudle s mákem *nood·leh smah·kehm*	wide noodles with poppy seeds, butter and sugar
nugát *noo·gaht*	nougat
obalovaný (ve strouhance) *oh·bah·loh·vah·nee (veh·stroh·hahn·tseh)*	breaded
oběd *oh·byeht*	lunch
obloha *ohb·loh·hah*	garnish
obložený chlebíček *ohb·loh·zheh·nee khleh·bee·chehk*	open sandwich
ocet *oh·tseht*	vinegar
okoun *oh·kohn*	perch
okurka *oh·koor·kah*	cucumber
olej *oh·lehy*	oil
oliva *oh·lih·vah*	olive
omáčka *oh·mahch·kah*	gravy, sauce
omeleta *oh·meh·leh·tah*	omelet
oplatek *ohp·lah·tehk*	wafer
ořech *oh·rzhehhk*	nut
ostružina *ohs·troo·zhih·nah*	blackberry
ostružinová marmeláda *ohs·troo·zhih·noh·vah mahr·meh·lah·dah*	blackberry jam
ostružinový koláč *ohs·troo·zhih·noh·vee koh·lahch*	blackberry pie
ostrý *ohst·ree*	hot (spicy)

ovesná kaše _oh_•vehs•_nah_ _kah_•sheh — oatmeal [porridge]

ovoc _oh_•vohts — fruit

ovoce z konzervy _oh_•voh•tseh _skohn_•zehr•vih — canned fruit

ovocný džus _oh_•vohts•**nee** dzhoos — fruit juice

ovocný koláč _oh_•vohts•**nee** koh•_lah_ch — fruit pie

ovocný kompot _oh_•vohts•**nee** _kohm_•poht — fruit compote

ovocný nápoj _oh_•vohts•**nee** _nah_•pohy — fruit drink

palačinka _pah_•lah•chihn•kah — thin pancake

palačinka s čokoládou _pah_•lah•chihn•kah _schoh_•koh•lah•doh — thin pancake with chocolate sauce

palačinka s ovocem a se zmrzlinou _pah_•lah•chihn•kah _soh_•voh•tsehm ah _seh_•zmrzlih•noh — thin pancake with fruit and ice cream

pálenka _pah_•lehn•kah — brandy

párek _pah_•rehk — thin sausage, made with finely ground pork

párek v rohlíku _pah_•rehk _vroh_•hl**ee**•koo — hot dog

paštika _pahsh_•tih•kah — pâté

pažitka _pah_•zhiht•kah — chives

pečená kachna _peh_•cheh•_nah_ _kahkh_•nah — roast duck

pečená ryba _peh_•cheh•_nah_ _rih_•bah — baked fish

pečeně _peh_·cheh·nyeh	roast
pečené kuře _peh_·cheh·neh _koo_·rzheh	roast chicken
pečeně se slaninou _peh_·cheh·neh _seh_·slah·nih·noh	roasted with bacon
pečený _peh_·cheh·nee	baked, roasted
pečený brambor _peh_·cheh·nee _brahm_·bohr	roast potato
pečivo _peh_·chih·voh	pastry
perlička _pehr_·lihch·kah	guinea fowl
perlivý _pehr_·lih·vee	carbonated
perník _pehr_·neek	gingerbread
petrželka _peht_·rzhehl·kah	parsley
pfeferonka _feh_·feh·rohn·kah	chili pepper
piškot _pihsh_·koht	sponge cake
pivo _pih_·voh	beer
plátek _plah_·tehk	slice
platýs _plah_·tees	halibut
plecko _plehts_·koh	shoulder (cut of meat)
plísňový sýr _plees_·n'oh·vee seer	blue cheese
plněné papriky v rajčatové omáčce _plnyeh_·neh pahp·rih·kih _vrahy_·chah·toh·veh _oh_·mahch·tseh	stuffed peppers in tomato sauce
plněný _plnyeh_·nee	stuffed
podmáslí _pohd_·mahs·lee	buttermilk
poleva _poh_·leh·vah	icing
polévka _poh_·lehf·kah	soup
pomazánka z Nivy _poh_·mah·zahn·kah _znih_·vih	blue cheese spread
pomeranč _poh_·meh·rahnch	orange
pomerančová marmeláda _poh_·meh·rahn·choh·vah mahr·meh·lah·dah	orange marmalade
pomerančový džus _poh_·meh·rahn·choh·vee dzhoos	orange juice

porce _pohr_·tseh	portion
pórek _poh_·rehk	leek
pórková polévka _pohr_·koh·vah _poh_·lehf·kah	leek soup
portské víno _pohrts_·keh vee·noh	port
pražený arašíd _prah_·zheh·nee ah·rah·sheed	roasted peanut
pražený mandle _prah_·zheh·nee mahnd·leh	roasted almond
prso prsoh	breast
předrkm przhehdkrm	appetizer
přírodní řízek _przhee_·rohd·nee _rzhee_·zehk	unbreaded cutlet
pstruh pstrooh	trout
pstruh na másle pstrooh nah·_mah_·sleh	trout fried with butter
pudink _poo_·dihnk	custard
pudinkový krém _poo_·dihn·koh·vee krehm	cream
punč poonch	punch
rajče _rahy_·cheh	tomato
rajská omáčka _rahy_·skah _oh_·mah·chkah	tomato sauce
rajská polévka _rahy_·skah _poh_·lehf·kah	tomato soup
rak rahk	crayfish
ramstejk _rahm_·stehyk	rumpsteak
rebarbora _reh_·bahr·boh·rah	rhubarb
rizoto _rih_·zoh·toh	risotto
rohlík _roh_·hleek	roll
rosol _roh_·sohl	aspic
roštěnka _rohsh_·tyehn·kah	sirloin steak
roštěnky na pivě _rohsh_·tyehn·kih _nah_·pih·vyeh	stew of beef and onion cooked in beer
rozinka _roh_·zihn·kah	raisin
rozmarýna _rohz_·mah·ree·nah	rosemary
ruláda _roo_·lah·dah	fillet steak
ruské vejce _roos_·keh _vehy_·tseh	eggs with mayonnaise

růžičková kapusta <u>roo</u>·zhihch·koh·**vah** kah·poos·tah	Brussels sprouts
růžový <u>roo</u>·zhoh·**vee**	rosé (wine)
ryba <u>rih</u>·bah	fish
rybí filé <u>rih</u>·bee <u>fih</u>·leh	fish fillet
rybí polévka <u>rih</u>·bee poh·**lehf**·kah	fish soup
rýže <u>ree</u>·zheh	rice
ředkvička <u>rzhehd</u>·kfihch·kah	radish
řeřicha <u>rzheh</u>·rzhih·khah	watercress
řízek <u>rzhee</u>·zehk	cutlet
s citrónem <u>stsih</u>·**troh**·nehm	with lemon
s cukrem <u>stsook</u>·rehm	with sugar
s ledem <u>sleh</u>·dehm	with ice
s mlékem <u>smleh</u>·kehm	with milk
salám <u>sah</u>·lahm	salami
salát <u>sah</u>·laht	salad, lettuce
salát ze syrového zelí <u>sah</u>·laht zeh <u>sih</u>·roh·**veh**·hoh <u>zeh</u>·lee	coleslaw
sardelky <u>sahr</u>·dehl·kih	anchovies
sardelová pasta <u>sahr</u>·deh·loh·**vah** pahs·tah	anchovy paste
sardinka <u>sahr</u>·dihn·kah	sardine

sekaná _seh_•kah•_nah_ — ground [minced] beef

selátko _seh_•_laht_•koh — suckling pig

sendvič _sehnd_•vihch — sandwich

sirup _sih_•roop — syrup

sklenice _skleh_•nih•tseh — glass

skopové _skoh_•poh•_veh_ — mutton

skopový guláš _skoh_•poh•_vee goo_•_lah_sh — mutton stew

skořice _skoh_•rzhih•tseh — cinnamon

skotská whisky _skoht_•skah _vihs_•kih — Scotch

sladkokyselá omáčka _slahd_•koh•kih•seh•_lah oh_•_mah_ch•kah — sweet-and-sour sauce

sladký _slahd_•kee — sweet

slané mandle _slah_•neh _mahn_•dleh — salted almond

slaneček _slah_•neh•chehk — salted herring

slanina _slah_•nih•nah — bacon

slaný _slah_•nee — salty

slávka _slahf_•kah — mussels

sleď _slehdy_ — herring

slepičí vývar s nudlemi _sleh_•pih•_chee vee_•vahr _snood_•leh•mih — chicken broth with noodles

slivovice _slih_•voh•vih•tseh — plum brandy

slunečnicová semínka _sloo_•nehch•nih•tsoh•_vah seh_•_meen_•kah — sunflower seeds

smažená ryba _smah_•zheh•_nah rih_•bah — fried fish

smažená vejce _smah_•zheh•_nah vehy_•tseh — scrambled eggs

smažené kuře _smah_•zheh•_neh koo_•rzheh — fried chicken

smaženka _smah_•zhehn•kah — croquette

smažený _smah_•zheh•_nee_ — fried

smažený kapr _smah_•zheh•_nee_ kahpr — carp fried in breadcrumbs

smažený květák s bramborem _smah_•zheh•_nee_ _kfyeh_•_tahk sbrahm_•boh•rehm — cauliflower fried in breadcrumbs

smažený sýr _smah_·zheh·_nee_ seer — cheese fried in breadcrumbs

smažený vepřový řízek _smah_·zheh·_nee_ _vehp_·rzhoh·_vee_ rzhee·zehk — fried pork chop Viennese style

smetana _smeh_·tah·nah — cream

smetanová omáčka _smeh_·tah·noh·_vah_ _oh_·**m**ahch·kah — cream sauce

smetanový _smeh_·tah·noh·_vee_ — creamy

sněhová pusinka _snyeh_·hoh·_vah_ _poo_·sihn·kah — meringue

snídaně _snee_·dah·nyeh — breakfast

sodovka _soh_·dohv·kah — soda water

sója _soh_·yah — soy [soya]

solený _soh_·leh·nee — salted

solený arašíd _soh_·leh·nee _ah_·rah·sheed — salted peanut

specialita dne _speh_·tsyah·lih·tah dneh — dish of the day

speciality šéfa kuchyně _speh_·tsyah·lih·tih _sheh_·fah _koo_·khih·nyeh — specialties of the house

srdce srtseh — heart

srnčí srnchee — venison

srnčí hřbet dušený na víně srnchee hrzhbeht _doo_·sheh·nee nah _vee_·nyeh — fillet of venison braised in wine

stehno _steh_·hnoh — leg (cut of meat)

stolní víno _stohl_·nee vee·noh — table wine

strouhanka _stroh_·hahn·kah — breadcrumbs

strouhaný _stroh_·hah·nee — grated

studená jídla _stoo_·deh·nah _yeed_·lah — cold dishes

studená polévka _stoo_·deh·nah poh·_lehf_·kah — cold soup

studená voda _stoo_·deh·nah _voh_·dah — iced water

studený _stoo_·deh·nee — cold

suchý _soo_·chee — dry

sůl sool — salt

sultánka _suhl·tahn·kah_	sultana raisin
sušená švestka _soo·sheh·nah shfehst·kah_	prune
sušené datle _soo·sheh·neh daht·leh_	dried date
sušenka _soo·shehn·kah_	cookie [biscuit]
sušený fík _soo·sheh·nee feek_	dried fig
svíčková _sveech·koh·vah_	tenderloin (cut of meat)
svíčková na smetaně _sveech·koh·vah nah·smeh·tah·nyeh_	beef tenderloin in creamy root vegetable sauce
sýr _seer_	cheese
syrový _sih·roh·vee_	raw
šafrán _shahf·rahn_	saffron
šalotka _shah·loht·kah_	shallot
šalvěj _shahl·vyehy_	sage
šery _sheh·rih_	sherry
šípkový čaj _sheep·koh·vee chahy_	rosehip tea
škubánky s mákem _shkoo·bahn·kih smah·kehm_	bread dumplings with poppy seeds and sugar
šlehačka _shleh·hahch·kah_	whipped cream
šopský salát _shohps·kee sah·laht_	tomato, cucumber and feta cheese salad
špagety _shpah·geh·tih_	spaghetti
špek _shpehk_	bacon
špekáčka _shpeh·kahch·kah_	thin sausage
špekový knedlík se zelím _shpeh·koh·vee knehd·leek seh·zeh·leem_	dumplings stuffed with bacon, served with sauerkraut
špenát _shpeh·naht_	spinach
šproty _shproh·tih_	sprats (small herring)
šťáva _sht'ah·vah_	gravy
štika _shtih·kah_	pike
štrúdl _shtroodl_	apple strudel

šumivé víno _shoo_•mih•v**eh** _vee_•noh	sparkling wine
šumivý _shoo_•mih•v**ee**	sparkling (drinks)
šunka _shoon_•kah	ham
šunka od kosti _shoon_•kah _oht_•kohs•tih	ham on the bone
šunka s vejci _shoon_•kah s**vehy**•tsih	ham and eggs
švestka _shfehst_•kah	plum
švestkové knedlíky _shfehst_•koh•v**eh** _knehd_•**lee**•kih	plum dumplings with curd cheese and sugar
tatarský biftek _tah_•tahrs•k**ee** _beef_•tehk	steak tartare
tavený sýr _tah_•veh•n**ee** s**eer**	soft cheese
telecí _teh_•leh•ts**ee**	veal
telecí játra _teh_•leh•ts**ee** _yah_•trah	veal liver
teplý _tehp_•l**ee**	warm
těsto _tyehs_•toh	pastry
těstoviny _tyehs_•toh•vih•nih	pasta
těžký _tyehzh_•k**ee**	full-bodied (wine)
tmavý chléb _tmah_•v**ee** khl**eh**b	dark bread
toast tohst	toast
tonik _toh_•nihk	tonic water
topinka _toh_•pihn•kah	toast
tresčí játra _trehs_•ch**ee** y**aht**•rah	cod liver

treska _trehs_•kah	cod
třešeň _trzheh_•shehn'	cherry
tučný _tooch_•nee	fatty
tuňák _too_•n'ahk	tuna
turecká káva _too_•rehts•**kah** kah•vah	Turkish coffee
tykev _tih_•kehf	squash
tymián _tih_•myahn	thyme
uherský salám _oo_•hehrs•**kee** sah•**lahm**	Hungarian salami
úhoř _oo_•horzh	eel
umělé sladidlo _oo_•myeh•leh _slah_•dih•dloh	sweetener
ústřice _oos_•trzhih•tseh	oyster
utopenci _oo_•toh•pehn•tsih	sausage marinated in vinegar
uzená makrela _oo_•zeh•**nah** mahk•reh•lah	smoked mackerel
uzená šunka _oo_•zeh•**nah** _shoon_•kah	smoked ham
uzenáč _oo_•zeh•**nahch**	smoked herring
uzené maso _oo_•zeh•**neh** mah•soh	smoked pork
uzené maso se zelím a knedlíky _oo_•zeh•**neh** mah•soh seh•zeh•**leem** ah•knehd•**lee**•kih	smoked pork with sauerkraut and dumplings
uzený _oo_•zeh•nee	smoked
uzený búček _oo_•zeh•nee _boo_•chehk	smoked pork bacon
uzený jazyk _oo_•zeh•nee _yah_•zihk	smoked tongue
uzený losos _oo_•zeh•nee _loh_•sohs	smoked salmon
uzený sýr _oo_•zeh•nee seer	smoked cheese
uzený úhoř _oo_•zeh•nee _oo_•hohrzh	smoked eel
vafle _vahf_•leh	waffle
vaječná jídla _vah_•yehch•nah yeed•lah	egg dishes
vanilka _vah_•nihl•kah	vanilla
vanilková zmrzlina _vah_•nihl•koh•**vah** _zmrzlih_•nah	vanilla ice cream

vařené brambory _vah_•rzheh•n**eh** _brahm_•boh•rih   boiled potatoes

vařený v páře _vah_•rzheh•n**ee** _fpah_•rzheh   steamed

vařící _vah_•rzhee•ts**ee**   boiling (water)

večeře _veh_•cheh•rzheh   dinner

vejce _vehy_•tseh   egg

vepřová klobáska _vehp_•rzhoh•v**ah** _kloh_•b**ah**s•kah   pork sausage

vepřové _vehp_•rzhoh•v**eh**   pork

vepřové žebírko _vehp_•rzhoh•v**eh** _zheh_•b**eer**•koh   stewed rib of pork

vermut _vehr_•moot   vermouth

vídeňská káva _vee_•dehn's•**kah** _kah_•vah   Viennese-style coffee topped with whipped cream

víno _vee_•noh   wine

višeň _vih_•shehn'   sour cherry

vlašský ořech _vlahsh_•skee _oh_•rzhehkh   walnut

voda _voh_•dah   water

vuřt voorzht   sausage

vývar _vee_•vahr   consommé

zajíc _zah_•y**ee**ts   hare

zajíc na divoko _zah_•y**ee**ts _nah_•dih•voh•koh   hare cooked with bacon, onions and vegetables in red wine

zajíc na smetaně _zah_•y**ee**ts _nah_•smeh•tah•nyeh   hare in rich cream sauce

zákusek _zah_•koo•sehk   cake, dessert

zapékaný _zah_•peh•kah•nee   au gratin

zavináč _zah_•vih•n**ah**ch   pickled herring [rollmop]

zázvor _zahz_•vohr   ginger

zázvorky _zahz_·vohr·kih — ginger cookies

zelená paprika _zeh_·leh·nah
pahp·rih·kah — green peppers

zeléňačka _zeh·leh·n'ahch·kah_ — thick soup with potatoes, sauerkraut and cream

zelené fazole _zeh·leh·neh_ _fah_·zoh·leh — green beans

zelenina _zeh_·leh·nih·nah — vegetable

zeleninová jídla _zeh_·leh·nih·noh·vah _yeed_·lah — vegetable dishes

zeleninová polévka _zeh_·leh·nih·noh·vah poh·**lehf**·kah — vegetable soup

zelí _zeh_·lee — cabbage

zelná polévka s klobásou _zehl_·nah poh·**lehf**·kah _skloh_·**bah**·soh — cabbage soup with smoked sausage

zmrzlina _zmrzlih_·nah — ice cream

zmrzlinový pohár (s ovocem) _zmrzlih_·noh·vee poh·**hahr** (_soh_·voh·tsehm) — ice-cream sundae (with fruit)

znojemská pečeně _znoh_·yehms·**kah** _peh_·cheh·nyeh — slices of roast beef in a pickle sauce

zralý _zrah_·lee — ripe

zvěřina _zvyeh_·rzhih·nah — game

žampion _zhahm_·pyohn — champignon mushroom

žebírka _zheh_·beer·kah — ribs

želé _zheh_·leh — jelly

žemle _zhehm_·leh — bun

žitný chléb _zhiht_·nee khl**eh**b — rye bread

žloutek _zhloh_·tehk — egg yolk

People

Conversation

ESSENTIAL

Hello./Hi!	**Dobrý den./Nazdar!**	_dohb•ree_ dehn/_nahz•_dahr
How are you?	**Jak se máte?**	yahk seh _mah•_teh
Fine, thanks.	**Dobře, děkuji.**	_dohb•_rzheh _dyeh•_koo•yih
Excuse me!	**Promiňte!**	_proh•_mihn'•teh
Do you speak English?	**Mluvíte anglicky?**	_mloo•vee•_teh _ahn•_glihts•kih
What's your name?	**Jak se jmenujete?**	yahk seh _ymeh•_noo•yeh•teh
My name is...	**Jmenuji se...**	_ymeh•_noo•yih seh...
Pleased to meet you.	**Těší mě.**	_tyeh•_shee myeh
Where are you from?	**Odkud jste?**	_oht•_koot ysteh
I'm from the U.S./ the U.K.	**Jsem ze Spojených Státú/z Velké Británie.**	ysehm _zeh•_spoh•yeh•neekh _stah•_too/_sfehl•keh_ brih•_tah•_nyeh
What do you do?	**Čím jste?**	cheem ysteh
I work for...	**Pracuji pro...**	_prah•_tsoo•yih proh...
I'm a student.	**Jsem student m/studentka f.**	ysehm _stoo•_dehnt/ _stoo•_dehnt•kah
I'm retired.	**Jsem v důchodu.**	ysehm _vdoo•_khoh•doo
Do you like...?	**Chcete...?**	_khtseh•_teh...
Goodbye.	**Na shledanou.**	_nahs•_hleh•dah•noh
See you later.	**Na viděnou.**	_nah•_vih•dyeh•noh

Language Difficulties

Do you speak English?	**Mluvíte anglicky?**	_mloo•vee•_teh _ahn•_glihts•kih
Does anyone here speak English?	**Mluví tady někdo anglicky?**	_mloo•vee_ tah•dih _nyehg•_doh _ahn•_glihts•kih
I don't speak much Czech.	**Neumím moc česky.**	_neh•_oo•meem mohts _chehs•_kih

Could you speak more slowly?	**Můžete mluvit pomaleji?** _moo_·zheh·teh _mloo_·viht _poh_·mah·leh·yih	
Could you repeat that?	**Můžete to zopakovat?** _moo_·zheh·teh toh zoh·pah·koh·vaht	
What was that?	**Co jste řekl?** tsoh ysteh rzhehkl	
Can you write it down?	**Můžete mi to napsat?** _moo_·zheh·teh mih toh _nahp_·saht	
Can you spell it?	**Můžete to vyhláskovat?** _moo_·zhe·hteh toh _vih_·hlaas·koh·vaht?	
Can you translate this for me?	**Můžete mi tohle přeložit?** _moo_·zheh·teh mih toh·hleh przheh·loh·zhiht	
What does this/that mean?	**Co to/tamto znamená?** tsoh toh/_tahm_·toh _znah_·meh·**nah**	

YOU MAY HEAR...

Mluvím jenom trochu anglicky. yeh·nohm troh·khoo ahn·glihts·kih

I only speak a little English.

Nemluvím anglicky. neh·mloo·**vee**m ahn·glihts·kih

I don't speak English.

Upon meeting, men generally shake hands—whether they are meeting for the first time or are old friends. Women shake hands with women and men at the first meeting or in formal situations. Kisses on the cheek are not commonly accepted in the Czech Republic; it is practiced only among close friends.

I understand.	**Rozumím.** _roh·zoo·meem_	
I don't understand.	**Nerozumím.** _neh·roh·zoo·meem_	
Do you understand?	**Rozumíte?** _roh·zoo·mee·teh_	

Making Friends

Hello./Hi!	**Dobrý den./Nazdar!** _dohb·ree dehn/ nahz·dahr_	
Good morning.	**Dobré ráno.** _dohb·reh rah·noh_	
Good afternoon.	**Dobré odpoledne.** _dohb·reh oht·poh·lehd·neh_	
Good evening.	**Dobrý večer.** _dohb·ree veh·chehr_	
My name is...	**Jmenuji se...** _ymeh·noo·yih seh..._	
What's your name?	**Jak se jmenujete?** _yahk seh ymeh·noo·yeh·teh_	
I'd like to introduce you to...	**Dovolte, abych Vám představil...** _doh·vohl·teh ah·bihkh vahm przhehd·stah·vihl..._	
Pleased to meet you.	**Těší mě.** _tyeh·shee myeh_	
How are you?	**Jak se máte?** _yahk seh mah·teh_	
Fine, thanks.	**Dobře, děkuji.** _dohb·rzheh dyeh·koo·yih_	
And you?	**A Vy?** _ah vih_	

Travel Talk

I'm here...	**Jsem zde...** _ysehm zdeh..._	
on business	**služebně** _sloo·zhehb·nyeh_	
on vacation [holiday]	**na dovolené** _nah·doh·voh·leh·neh_	

studying	**studuji** _stoo_•doo•yih	
I'm staying for...	**Budu tady...** _boo_•doo _tah_•dih...	
I've been here...	**Jsem tady...** ysehm _tah_•dih...	
a day	**na den** _nah_•dehn	
a week	**na týden** _nah_•tee•dehn	
a month	**na měsíc** _nah_•myeh•**see**ts	
Where are you from?	**Odkud jste?** _oht_•koot ysteh	
I'm from...	**Jsem z...** ysehm s...	

For Numbers, see page 175.

Personal

Who are you with?	**S kým tady jste?** skeem _tah_•dih ysteh	
I'm on my own.	**Jsem tady sám** _m_/**sáma** _f._ ysehm _tah_•dih s**ah**m/ _sah_•mah	
I'm with...	**Jsem tady s...** ysehm _tah_•dih s...	
my husband/ wife	**manželem/manželkou** _mahn_•zheh•lehm/ _mahn_•zhehl•koh	
my boyfriend/ girlfriend	**milencem/milenkou** _mih_•lehn•tsehm/_mih_•lehn•koh	
a friend/ colleague	**přítelem/kolegou** _przhee_•teh•lehm/_koh_•leh•goh	

When's your birthday?	**Kdy máte narozeniny?** *ghih <u>mah</u>•teh <u>nah</u>•roh•zeh•nih•nih*
How old are you?	**Kolik je vám let?** *<u>koh</u>•lihk yeh vahm leht*
I'm…	**Mne…letý.** *mneh…<u>leh</u>•tee*
Are you married?	**Jste** *ženatý m/***vdaná** *f?* *ysteh <u>zheh</u>•nah•tee/ <u>vdah</u>•nah*
I'm in a relationship.	**Jsem ve vztahu.** *ysem veh vstah•hoo*
I'm…	**Jsem…** *ysehm…*
single	**svobodný** *m/***svobodná** *f <u>sfoh</u>•bohd•nee/ <u>sfoh</u>•bohd•nah*
married	**ženatý** *m/***vdaná** *f <u>zheh</u>•nah•tee/vdah•nah*
engaged	**zasnoubený/á** *zahs•no•oo•ben•nee*
divorced	**rozvedený** *m/***rozvedená** *f <u>rohz</u>•veh•deh•nee/ <u>rohz</u>•veh•deh•nah*
I'm separated.	**Jsem v separaci.** *ysehm <u>fseh</u>•pah•rah•tsih*
I'm in a relationship.	**Mám partnera** *m/***partnerku** *f. mahm <u>pahrt</u>•neh•rah/<u>pahrt</u>•nehr•koo*
I'm widowed.	**Jsem vdovec** *m/***vdova** *f. ysehm <u>vdoh</u>•vehts/ <u>vdoh</u>•vah*
Do you have children/ grandchildren?	**Máte děti/vnuky?** *<u>mah</u>•teh dyeh•tih/<u>vnoo</u>•kih*

Work & School

What do you do?	**Čím jste?** *cheem ysteh*
What are you studying?	**Co studujete?** *tsoh <u>stoo</u>•doo•yeh•teh*
I'm studying…	**Studuji…** *<u>stoo</u>•doo•yih…*
I work full time/ part time.	**Pracuji v plném/v polovičním úvazku.** *<u>prah</u>•tsoo•yih fplnehm/<u>fpoh</u>•loh•vihch•neem oo•vahs•koo*
Who do you work for?	**Pro koho pracujete?** *proh <u>koh</u>•hoh <u>prah</u>•tsoo•yeh•teh*

I work for. . .	**Pracuji pro. . .** _prah•tsoo•yih proh_. . .
I am unemployed.	**Jsem nezaměstnaný/á.** _Sem neh•zah•mnyest•nah•nee_
I work at home.	**Pracuji z domova.** _Prah•tsoo•yih z doh•moh•vah._
Here's my business card.	**Zde je moje vizitka.** _zdeh yeh moh•yeh vih•ziht•kah_

For Grammar, see page 167.

Weather

What's the weather forecast for tomorrow?	**Jaká je předpověď počasí na zítřek?** _yah•kah yeh przheht•poh•vyehty poh•chah•see nah•zeet•rzhehk_
What beautiful/ terrible weather!	**Jaké krásné/ošklivé počasí!** _yah•keh krahs•neh/ ohsh•klih•veh poh•chah•see_
It's cool/warm.	**Je chladno/teplo.** _yeh khlahd•noh/tehp•loh_
It's cold/hot.	**Je zima/horko.** _Yeh zih•mah/hohr•koh._
It's rainy/sunny.	**Je deštivě/sluneční počasí.** _yeh dehsh•tih•vyeh/ sloo•nehch•nee poh•chah•see_
It's snowy.	**Sněží.** _snyeh•zhee_
It's icy.	**Je zima.** _yeh zih•mah_
Do I need a jacket/ an umbrella?	**Budu potřebovat bundu/deštník?** _boo•doo poht•rzheh•boh•vaht boon•doo/dehsht•neek_

For Temperature, see page 181.

ESSENTIAL

Would you like to go out for a drink/meal?	**Nešli bychom si dát drink/jídlo?** _nesh_•lih _bih_•khohm sih d**ah**t drihnk/_jeed_•loh
What are your plans for tonight/tomorrow?	**Jaké máte plány na dnešní večer/zítřek?** _yah_•k**eh** _mah_•teh _plah_•nih nah _dnehsh_•nee _veh_•chehr/ _zeet_•rzhehk
Can I have your number?	**Dáte mi Vaše telefonní číslo?** _dah_•teh mih _vah_•sheh _teh_•leh•fohn•nee _chees_•loh
Can I join you?	**Můžu se přisednout?** _moo_•hoo seh _przhih_•sehd•noht
Can I buy you a drink?	**Mohu Vám objednat něco k pití?** _moh_•hoo v**ah**m _ohb_•yehd•naht _nyeh_•tsoh _kpih_•tee
I like you.	**Mám tě rád m/ráda f.** m**ah**m tyeh rahd/_rah_•dah
I love you.	**Miluji tě.** _mih_•loo•yih tyeh

The Dating Game

Would you like to go out for coffee/ dinner?	**Nešli bychom na kávu/večeři?** _nehsh_•lih _bih_•khohm _nah_•kah•voo/_veh_•cheh•rzhih
What are your plans for...?	**Jaké máte plány na...?** _yah_•k**eh** _mah_•teh _plah_•nih nah...
today	**dnes** _dnehs_
tonight	**dnešní večer** _dnehsh_•nee _veh_•chehr
tomorrow	**zítřek** _zeet_•rzhehk
this weekend	**víkend** _vee_•kehnd

Where would you like to go?	**Kam by si chtěl jít?** *kahm bih sih khtyehl yeet*
I'd like to go to...	**Chtěl *m*/Chtěla *f* bych jít do...** *khtyehl/khtyeh·lah bihkh yeet doh...*
Do you like...?	**Chcete...?** *khtseh·teh...*
Can I have your number/email?	**Dáte mi Vaše telefonní číslo/adresu elektronické pošty?** *dah·teh mih vah·sheh teh·leh·fohn·nee chees·loh/ahd·reh·soo eh·lehk·troh·nihts·keh pohsh·tih*
Are you on Facebook/Twitter?	**Máš účet na Facebooku/Twitteru?** *Maash oo·tchet nah Face·boo·koo/Twi·tte·roo?*
Can I join you?	**Můžu se přisednout?** *moo·zhoo seh przhih·sehd·noh*
You're very attractive.	**Vypadáte báječně.** *vih·pah·dah·teh bah·yehch·nyeh*
Shall we go somewhere quieter?	**Půjdeme někam kde je větší klid?** *pooy·deh·meh nyeh·kahm gdeh yeh vyeht·shee klihd*

Accepting & Rejecting

Thank you. I'd love to.	**Děkuji. Velice rád *m*/ráda *f*.** *dyeh·koo·yih veh·lih·tseh raht/rah·dah*
Where shall we meet?	**Kde se setkáme?** *gdeh seh seht·kah·meh*
I'll meet you at the bar/your hotel.	**Sejdeme se v baru/ve vašem hotelu.** *sehy·deh·meh seh fbah·roo/veh·vah·shehm hoh·teh·loo*

I'll come by at...	**Přijdu v...** _przhihy_•doo v...
What's your address?	**Kde bydlíte?** _gdeh bihd•lee•teh_
I'm busy.	**Jsem zaneprázdněný** _m_/**zaneprázdněná** _f._ _ysehm_ _zah•nehp•rah_zd•nyeh•nee/_zah•nehp•rah_zd•nyeh•nah
I'm not interested.	**Nemám zájem.** _neh•mahm zah•yehm_
Leave me alone, please.	**Nechte mí, prosím.** _nekh•teh mee proh•seem_
Stop bothering me!	**Ne otravujte mně!** _neh oht•rah•vooy•teh mnyeh_

Getting Intimate

Can I hug/kiss you?	**Můžu se k tobě přitisknout/tě políbit?** _moo•zhoo seh ktoh•byeh przhih•tihs•knoht/tyeh poh•lee•biht_
Yes.	**Ano.** _ah•noh_
No.	**Ne.** _neh_
Stop!	**Nech toho!** _nehkh toh•hoh_
I love you.	**Miluji tě.** _Mih•loo•yih tyeh_

Sexual Preferences

Are you gay?	**Jseš homosexual?** _ysehsh hoh•moh•seh•ksoo•ahl_
I'm...	**Jsem...** _ysehm..._
heterosexual	**heterosexuální** _m_/**heterosexuálná** _f_ _heh•teh•roh•seh•ksoo•ahl•nee/_ _heh•teh•roh•seh•ksoo•ahl•nah_
homosexual	**homosexuální** _m_/**homosexuálná** _f_ _hoh•moh•seh•ksoo•ahl•nee/_ _hoh•moh•seh•ksoo•ahl•nah_
bisexual	**bisexuální** _m_/**bisexuálná** _f_ _bih•seh•ksoo•ahl•nee/bih•seh•ksoo•ahl•nah_
Let's go to a gay bar/club.	**Pojďme do gay baru/klubu.**

Leisure Time

ESSENTIAL

Where's the tourist information office?	**Kde je turistická kancelář?** _gdeh yeh_ _too·rihs·tihts·kah kahn·tseh·lah_rzh
What are the main points of interest?	**Co tady stojí za prohlédnutí?** _tsoh tah·dih stoh·yee zah proh·hlehd·noo·tee_
Are there tours in English?	**Jsou prohlídky s anglickým průvodcem?** _ysoh proh·hleet·kih sahn·glihts·keem proo·voht·tsehm_
Could I have a map/guide?	**Můžete mi dát mapu/průvodce?** _moo·zheh·teh mih daht mah·poo/proo·vohd·tseh_

Tourist Information

Do you have any information on...?	**Máte nějaké informace o...?** _mah·teh nyeh·yah·keh ihn·fohr·mah·tseh oh..._
Can you recommend...?	**Můžete mi doporučit...?** _moo·zheh·teh mih doh·poh·roo·chiht..._
a boat trip	**výlet lodí** _vee·leht loh·dee_
an excursion	**výlet** _vee·leht_
a sightseeing tour	**prohlídku** _proh·hleet·koo_
a tour of...	**výlet po...** _vee·leht poh..._

Turistické kanceláře (tourist information offices) are usually located in the vicinity of train stations or in city centers. They are open from Monday to Friday and, during the tourist season, also on Saturday and Sunday. Opening hours vary. Visit **czechtourism.com** for more information.

On Tour

I'd like to go on the tour to…	**Mám zájem o zájezd do…** mahm <u>zah</u>-yehm oh <u>zah</u>-yehzd doh…
When's the next tour?	**Kdy bude další zájezd?** gdyh <u>boo</u>-deh <u>dahl</u>-shee <u>zah</u>-yezd
Are there tours in English?	**Jsou zájezdy s anglickým průvodcem?** ysoh <u>zah</u>-yehz-dih <u>sahn</u>-glihts-k<u>ee</u>m <u>proo</u>-voht-tsehm
Is there an English-speaking guide?	**Máte průvodce, kteří umí anglicky?** <u>mah</u>-teh <u>proo</u>-voht-tseh <u>kteh</u>-rzh<u>ee</u> <u>oo</u>-mee <u>ahn</u>-glihts-kih
Is there an English guide book/audio guide?	**Máte průvodce/audioprůvodce v angličtině?** <u>Mah</u>-teh <u>proo</u>-vod-tse/<u>ow</u>-deeoh-<u>proo</u>-vod-tse <u>fahn</u>-glihtsch-tji-njeh?
What time do we leave/return?	**V kolik vyrazíme/se vrátíme?** <u>fkoh</u>-lik <u>vih</u>-rah-zee-meh/seh <u>vrah</u>-tee-meh
We'd like to see…	**Rádi bychom viděli…** <u>rah</u>-dih <u>bih</u>-khohm <u>vih</u>-dyeh-lih…
Can we stop here…?	**Mohli bychom tady zastavit na…?** <u>moh</u>-hlih <u>bih</u>-khohm <u>tah</u>-dih <u>zahs</u>-tah-viht nah…
to take photographs	**pár fotek** <u>pah</u>r <u>foh</u>-tehk
to buy souvenirs	**nákup suvenýrů** <u>nah</u>-koop <u>soo</u>-veh-nee-roo
to use the restrooms [toilets]	**záchod** <u>zah</u>-khoht
Is there access for the disabled?	**Je přístup pro invalidy?** yeh <u>przhee</u>-stoop proh-<u>ihn</u>-vah-lih-dih

For Tickets, see page 18.

Seeing the Sights

Where is/are…?	**Kde je/jsou…?** gdeh yeh/ysoh…
the battleground	**bitevní pole** <u>bih</u>-tehv-nee <u>poh</u>-leh

the botanical garden	**botanická zahrada** _boh_·tah·nihts·**kah** zah·hrah·dah
the castle	**hrad** hraht
the downtown area	**centrum** tsehn·troom
the fountain	**kašna** kahsh·nah
the library	**knihovna** knih·hohv·nah
the market	**tržnice** trzhnih·tseh
the museum	**muzeum** moo·zeh·oom
the old town	**staré město** stah·reh myehs·toh
the opera house	**budova opery** boo·do·vah oh·peh·ry
the palace	**palác** pah·lahts
the park	**park** pahrk
the ruins	**zříceniny** zrzhee·tseh·nih·nih
the shopping area	**nákupní centrum** nah·koop·nee tsehnt·room
the town square	**náměstí** nah·myehs·tee
Can you show me on the map?	**Můžete mi to ukázat na mapě?** moo·zheh·teh mih toh oo·kah·zaht nah·mah·pyeh
It's…	**To je…** toh yeh…
amazing	**obdivuhodné** ohb·dih·voo·hohd·neh
beautiful	**krásné** krahs·neh

boring	**nudné** <u>nood</u>·neh
interesting	**zajímavé** <u>zah</u>·yee·mah·veh
magnificent	**velkolepé** <u>vehl</u>·koh·leh·peh
romantic	**romantické** <u>roh</u>·mahn·tihts·keh
strange	**divné** <u>dihv</u>·neh
stunning	**skvělé** <u>skfyeh</u>·leh
terrible	**strašné** <u>strahsh</u>·neh
ugly	**ošklivé** <u>ohsh</u>·klih·veh
I like/don't like it.	**Líbí/Nelíbí se mi to.** <u>lee</u>·bee/<u>neh</u>·lee·bee seh mih toh

Religious Sites

Where's…?	**Kde je…?** gdeh yeh…
the cathedral	**katedrála** <u>kah</u>·tehd·rah·lah
the Catholic/	**katolický/evangelický kostel** <u>kah</u>·toh·lihts·kee/
Protestant church	<u>eh</u>·vahn·geh·lihts·kee <u>kohs</u>·tehl
the mosque	**mešita** <u>meh</u>·shih·tah
the shrine	**kaple** <u>kahp</u>·leh
the synagogue	**synagóga** <u>sih</u>·nah·goh·gah
the temple	**chrám** khrahm
What time is mass/	**V kolik hodin je mše/bohoslužba?** <u>fkoh</u>·lihk
the service?	<u>hoh</u>·dihn yeh msheh/<u>boh</u>·hoh·sloozh·bah

ESSENTIAL

Where is the market/mall?	**Kde je tržnice/nákupní centrum?**	_gdeh yeh trzhnih•tseh/nah•koop•nee tsehnt•room_
I'm just looking.	**Jenom se dívám.**	_yeh•nohm seh dee•vahm_
Can you help me?	**Můžete mi pomoci?**	_moo•zheh•teh mih poh•moh•tsih_
I'm being helped.	**Již mě obsluhují.**	_yihzh myeh ohp•sloo•hoo•yee_
How much?	**Kolik?**	_koh•lihk_
That one.	**Tamten.**	_tahm•tehn_
That's all, thanks.	**To je všechno, děkuji.**	_toh yeh vsheh•khnoh dyeh•koo•yih_
Where do I pay?	**Kde zaplatím?**	_gdeh zah•plah•teem_
I'll pay in cash/by credit card.	**Zaplatím v hotovosti/kreditní kartou.**	_zah•plah•teem fhoh•toh•voh•stih/kreh•diht•nee kahr•toh_
A receipt, please.	**Stvrzenku, prosím.**	_stvrzehn•koo proh•seem_

At the Shops

Where is…?	**Kde je/jsou…?**	_gdeh yeh/ysoh…_
the antiques store	**starožitností**	_stah•roh•zhiht•nohs•tee_
the bakery	**pekařství**	_peh•kahrzh•stfee_
the bank	**banka**	_bahn•kah_
bookstore	**knihkupectví**	_knihh•koo•pehts•tfee_
the clothing store	**oděvy**	_oh•dyeh•vih_
the delicatessen	**lahůtky**	_lah•hoot•kih_
the department store	**obchodní dům**	_ohp•khohd•nee doom_

YOU MAY HEAR…

Čím posloužím? *cheem pohs·loh·zheem*		Can I help you?
Chviličku. *khfih·lihch·koo*		One moment.
Co byste si přáli? *tsoh bihs·teh sih przhah·lih*		What would you like?
Ještě něco? *yehsh·tyeh nyeh·tsoh*		Anything else?

the gift shop	**suvenýry** *soo·veh·nee·rih*	
the health food store	**zdravá výživa** *zdrah·vah vee·zhih·vah*	
the jeweler	**klenotnictví** *kleh·noht·nihts·tfee*	
the liquor store [off-licence]	**obchod lihovinami** *ohp·khohd lih·hoh·vih·nah·mih*	
the market	**tržnice** *trzhnih·tseh*	
the pastry shop	**cukrárna** *tsook·rahr·nah*	
the pharmacy [chemist]	**lékárna** *leh·kahr·nah*	
the produce [grocery] store	**potraviny** *poht·rah·vih·nih*	
the shoe store	**obuvnictví** *oh·boov·nihts·tfee*	
the shopping mall [centre]	**nákupní centrum** *nah·koop·nih tsehnt·room*	

In some major chain stores such as **Delvita**, euro (notes only) are accepted, as are of course **korun** (Czech crowns). Credit cards are accepted by all major shops and the majority of restaurants. However, in restaurants it is advisable to check the minimum amount accepted for payment by card.

YOU MAY SEE...

OTEVŘENO/ZAVŘENO	open/closed
UZAVŘENA NA OBĚD	closed for lunch
ZKUŠEBNÍ KABINA	fitting room
POKLADNÍ	cashier
POUZE V HOTOVOSTI	cash only
AKCEPTACE KREDITNÍCH KARET	credit cards accepted
WC/TOALETY	restrooms
VÝCHOD	exit

the souvenir store	**suvenýry**	_soo_•veh•**nee**•rih
the supermarket	**samoobsluha**	_sah_•moh•ohp•sloo•hah
the tobacconist	**tabák**	_tah_•**bahk**
the toy store	**hračkářství**	_hrahch_•**kah**rzh•stf**ee**

Ask an Assistant

When does... open/close?	**Kdy...otvírá/zavírá?**	_gdih_...**oht**•fee•rah/_zah_•vee•rah
Where is/are...?	**Kde je/jsou...?**	_gdeh yeh/ysoh..._
the cashier [cash desk]	**pokladna**	_pohk_•lahd•nah
the escalator	**eskalátor**	_ehs_•kah•**lah**•tohr
the elevator [lift]	**výtah**	_vee_•tah
the fitting rooms	**zkušební kabinka**	_skoo_•shehb•nee **kah**•bihn•kah
the store directory	**informační tabule**	_ihn_•fohr•mahch•nee **tah**•boo•leh
Can you help me?	**Můžete mi pomoci?**	_moo_•zheh•teh mih _poh_•moh•tsih
I'm just looking.	**Jenom se dívám.**	_yeh_•nohm seh **dee**•vahm
I'm being helped.	**Už mě obsluhují.**	_oozh_ myeh **ohb**•sloo•hoo•yee
Do you have any...?	**Máte...?**	_mah_•teh...

Can you show me…?	**Můžete mi ukázat…?** _moo_·zheh·teh mih _oo_·**kah**·zaht…
Can you ship/wrap it?	**Můžete mi to poslat/zabalit?** _moo_·zheh·teh mih toh _pohs_·laht/_zah_·bah·liht
How much?	**Kolik?** _koh_·lihk
That's all, thanks.	**To je všechno, děkuji.** toh yeh _fshehkh_·noh _dyeh_·koo·yih

For Clothing, see page 125.

Personal Preferences

I'd like something…	**Chtěl** _m_/**Chtěla** _f_ **bych něco…** khtyehl/_khtyeh_·lah bihkh _n'eh_·tsoh…
cheap/expensive	**levného/drahého** _lehv_·neh·hoh/_drah_·heh·hoh
larger/smaller	**většího/menšího** _vyeht_·shee·hoh/_mehn_·shee·hoh
from this region	**místního** _mees_·tnee·hoh
Around…crown.	**Asi … korun.** _Ah_·sih … _koh_·roon
Is it real?	**Je to pravé?** yeh toh _prah_·veh
Could you show me this/that?	**Můžete mi ukázat tenhle/tamten?** _moo_·zheh·teh mih _oo_·**kah**·zaht _tehn_·hleh/_tahm_·tehn
That's not quite what I want.	**Není to úplně ono.** _neh_·nee toh _oopl_·nyeh _oh_·noh
No, I don't like it.	**Ne, to se mi nelíbí.** neh toh seh mih _neh_·**lee**·bee
That's too expensive.	**To je moc drahé.** toh yeh mohts _drah_·heh
I'd like to think about it.	**Ještě si to rozmyslím.** _yesh_·tyeh sih toh _rohz_·mihs·**leem**
I'll take it.	**Vezmu si to.** _vehz_·moo sih toh

For Souvenirs, see page 130.

Paying & Bargaining

How much?	**Kolik?** _koh_·lihk
I'll pay...	**Zaplatím...** _zah_·plah·teem...
in cash	**hotově** _hoh_·toh·vyeh
by credit card	**kreditní kartou** _kreh_·diht·nee _kahr_·toh
by travelers check [cheque]	**cestovním šekem** _tsehs_·tohv·neem _sheh_·kehm
A receipt, please.	**Stvrzenku, prosím.** _stvrzehn_·koo _proh_·seem
That's too much.	**Je to příliš drahé.** yeh toh _przhih_·leesh _drah_·heh
I'll give you...	**Dám vám...** _dahm_ vahm...
I only have...crowns.	**Mám jenom...korun.** mahm _yeh_·nohm... _koh_·roon
Is that your best price?	**To je nejnižší cena?** toh yeh _nehy_·nihzh·shee _tseh_·nah
Can you give me a discount?	**Dáte mi nějakou slevu?** _dah_·teh mih _nyeh_·yah·koh _sleh_·voo

For Numbers, see page 175.

YOU MAY HEAR...

Jak budete platit? yahk _boo_·deh·teh _plah_·tiht	How are you paying?
Vaše platební karta byla odmítnuta. _Vah_·she _plah_·tehb·nyee _kahr_·tah bih·lah _od_·meet·noo·tah	Your (credit) card has been declined.
Prosím Váš doklad totožnosti. _Proh_·seem vaash _dok_·lahd _toh_·tozh·nos·tyi	ID, please.
Nepřijímáme kreditní karty. _Neh_·przi·yee·maah·meh _kreh_·dit·nyee _kahr_·ty	We don't accept credit cards.
Jenom v hotovostí, prosím. _yeh_·nohm _fhoh_·toh·voh·stee _proh_·seem	Cash only, please.
Nemáte menší drobné? _neh_·maah·teh _mehn_·shee _drohb_·neh	Do you have any smaller change?

Making a Complaint

I'd like...	**Chtěl** m/**Chtěla** f **bych...** khtyehl/khtyeh·lah bihkh...
to exchange this	**to vyměnit** toh vih·myeh·niht
to return this	**to vrátit** toh vrah·tiht
a refund	**vrátit peníze** vrah·tiht peh·nee·zeh
to see the manager	**mluvit s vedoucím** mloo·viht sfeh·doh·tseem

Services

Can you recommend...?	**Můžete mi doporučit...?** moo·zheh·teh mih doh·poh·roo·chiht...
a barber	**holičství** hoh·lihch·stfee
a dry cleaner	**čistírna** chihs·teer·nah
a hairdresser	**kadeřnictví** kah·dehrzh·nihts·tfee
a Laundromat [launderette]	**prádelna** prah·dehl·nah
a nail salon	**manikúru** mah·nih·koo·roo
a spa	**spa** spah
a travel agency	**cestovní kancelář** tsehs·tohv·nee kahn·tseh·lahrzh
Can you...this?	**Můžete to...?** moo·zheh·teh toh...
alter	**upravit** oo·prah·viht
clean	**vyčistit** vih·chihs·tiht
fix	**spravit** sprah·viht
press	**vyžehlit** vih·zheh·hliht
When will it be ready?	**Kdy to bude hotové?** gdih toh boo·deh hoh·toh·veh

Hair & Beauty

I'd like...	**Chtěl** m/**Chtěla** f **bych...** khtyehl/khtyeh·lah bihkh...
an appointment for today/tomorrow.	**termín na dnes/zítřek.** tehr·meen nah dnehs/zeet·rzehk
some color	**obarvit vlasy** oh·bahr·viht vlah·sih

Czech spas are characterized by luxurious facilities, a high level of service and, often, mineral springs. Among the most popular destinations are the southwestern **Karlové Vary** and **Mariánské Lázně**. **Luhačovice** and **Klimkovice** attract spa lovers to the region of **Moravia**, while **Karlova Studánka** in the heart of the **Jesionniki mountains** boasts the cleanest air in Central Europe.

some highlights	**melír** _meh_•l**ee**r	
my hair styled	**učesat** _oo_•cheh•saht	
my hair blow-dried	**provést styling vlasů vysoušečem**	
a haircut	**ostříhat** _ohs_•trzh**ee**•haht	
a trim	**zastřihnout** _zah_•strzhih•noht	
Don't cut it too short.	**Nestříhejte mě moc nakrátko.** _nehs_•trzh**ee**•hehy•teh meyh mohts _nah_•kr**aht**•koh	
Shorter here.	**Tady krátší.** _tah_•dih kr**aht**•sh**ee**	
I'd like...	**Chtěl** m/**Chtěla** f **bych...** khtyehl/_khtyeh_•lah bihkh...	
an eyebrow/ bikini wax	**depilaci obočí/bikiny voskem** _deh_•pih•lah•tsih _oh_•boh•ch**ee**/_bih_•kih•nih _vohs_•kehm	
a facial	**ošetřit obličej** _oh_•sheht•rzhiht _ohb_•lih•chehy	
a manicure/ pedicure	**manikúru/pedikúru** _mah_•nih•k**oo**•roo/ _peh_•dih•k**oo**•roo	
a (sports) massage	**(sportovní) masáž** (_spohr_•tohv•n**ee**) _mah_•s**ah**zh	
Do you do...?	**Děláte...?** _dyeh_•l**ah**•teh...	
acupuncture	**akupunkturu** _ah_•koo•poon•ktoo•roo	
aromatherapy	**aromatickou terapii** _ah_•roh•mah•tihts•koh _teh_•rah•pyih	

oxygen treatment	**kyslíkovou terapii** _kihs_•_lee_•koh•voh teh•rah•pyih
threading	**depilaci pomocí bavlněné nitě?** _deh_•pih•lah•tsi _poh_•moh•tsee _bah_•vl•nye•neh _nyi_•tye?
Is there a sauna?	**Je tady sauna?** yeh _tah_•dih _sow_•nah

Antiques

How old is this?	**Jak je to staré?** yahk yeh toh _stah_•**reh**
Do you have anything from the…era?	**Máte něco z…období?** _mah_•teh _nyeh_•tsoh z… _ohb_•doh•**bee**
Will I have problems with customs?	**Budu mít problémy na celnici?** _boo_•doo m**eet** _prohb_•**leh**•mih nah•_tsehl_•nih•tsih
Is there a certificate of authenticity?	**Máte osvědčení pravosti?** _mah_•teh _ohs_•fyeht•cheh•n**ee** _prah_•vohs•tih
Can you ship/wrap it?	**Můžete to poslat/zabalit?** _Moo_•zhe•teh toh _pohs_•laht/_zah_•bah•lit

---

YOU MAY SEE…

PÁNSKÉ ODĚVY	men's clothing
ŽENSKÉ ODĚVY	women's clothing
DĚTSKÉ ODĚVY	children's clothing

YOU MAY HEAR...

Vypadáte v tom skvěle! _Vyh•pah•daa•teh f tohm skvye•leh_   That looks great on you!

Pasuje to? _Pah•soo•yeh toh?_   How does it fit?

Nemáme vaši velikost. _Neh•maah•meh vah•shi veh•lih•kohst_   We don't have your size.

Clothing

I'd like...	**Chtěl** m/**Chtěla** f **bych...** _khtyehl/khtyeh•lah bihkh..._	
Can I try this on?	**Mohu si to zkusit?** _moh•hoo sih toh skoo•siht_	
It doesn't fit.	**Není mi to dobře.** _neh•nee mih toh dohb•rzheh_	
It's too...	**Je to moc...** _yeh toh mohts..._	
big/small	**velké/malé** _vehl•keh/mah•leh_	
short/long	**krátké/dlouhé** _kraht•keh/dloh•heh_	
tight/loose	**těsné/volné** _tyes•neh/vohl•neh_	
Do you have this in size...?	**Máte to ve velikosti...?** _mah•teh toh veh•veh•lih•kohs•tih..._	
Do you have this in a bigger/smaller size?	**Máte to v větší/menší velikosti?** _mah•teh toh vvyeht•shee/mehn•shee veh•lih•kohs•tih_	

For Numbers, see page 175.

Colors

I'd like something in...	**Chtěl** m/**Chtěla** f **bych něco...** _khtyehl/khtyeh•lah bihkh nyeh•tsoh..._	
beige	**béžový** _beh•zhoh•vee_	
black	**černý** _chehr•nee_	
blue	**modrý** _mohd•ree_	
brown	**hnědý** _hnyeh•dee_	

gray	**šedý**	_sheh_·dee
green	**zelený**	_zeh_·leh·nee
orange	**oranžový**	_oh_·rahn·zhoh·vee
pink	**růžový**	_roo_·zhoh·vee
purple	**fialový**	_fyah_·loh·vee
red	**červený**	_chehr_·veh·nee
white	**bílý**	_bee_·lee
yellow	**žlutý**	_zhloo_·tee

Clothes & Accessories

backpack	**batoh**	_bah_·toh
belt	**pásek**	_pah_·sehk
bikini	**bikiny**	_bih_·kih·nih
blouse	**blůza**	_bloo_·zah
bra	**podprsenka**	_poht_·prsehn·kah
briefs [underpants] panties [ladies]	**spodní kalhotky**	_spohd_·nee kahl·hoht·kih
coat	**kabát**	_kah_·baht
dress	**šaty**	_shah_·tih
hat	**klobouk**	_kloh_·bohk
jacket	**sako**	_sah_·koh
jeans	**džíny**	_dzhee_·nih
pyjamas	**pyžamo**	_pih_·zhah·moh
pants [trousers]	**kalhoty**	_kahl_·hoh·tih
pantyhose [tights]	**punčochové kalhoty**	_poon_·choh·khoh·veh _kahl_·hoh·tih
purse [handbag]	**kabelka**	_kah_·behl·kah
raincoat	**pláštěnka**	_plah_·shtyehn·kah
scarf	**šátek**	_shah_·tehk
shirt	**košile m/bluzka f**	_koh_·shih·leh/_bloo_·skah
shorts	**krátké kalhoty**	_kraht_·keh _kahl_·hoh·tih

skirt	**sukně** _sook_•nyeh
socks	**ponožky** _poh_•nohzh•kih
stockings	**punčochy** _poon_•choh•khih
suit	**oblek** m/**kostým** f _ohb_•lek/_kohs_•teem
sunglasses	**sluneční brýle** _sloo_•nehch•nee _bree_•leh
sweater	**svetr** sfehtr
sweatshirt	**tričko** _trihch_•koh
swimming trunks	**pánské plavky** _pahn_•skeh plahf•kih
swimsuit	**dámské plavky** _dahm_•skeh plahf•kih
T-shirt	**triko** _trih_•koh
tie	**kravata** _krah_•vah•tah
underwear	**spodní prádlo** _spohd_•nee prahd•loh

Fabric

I'd like…	**Chtěl** m/**Chtěla** f **bych něco…** khtyehl/_khtyeh_•lah bihkh _nyeh_•tsoh…
cotton	**z bavlny** _zbah_•vlnih
denim	**z džínsoviny** _zdzheen_•soh•vih•nih
lace	**z krajky** _skrahy_•kih
leather	**z kůže** _skoo_•zheh
linen	**ze lnu** _zeh_•lnoo

silk	**z hedvábí** _s hehd·vah·bee_
wool	**z vlny** _zvlnih_
Is it machine washable?	**Pere se to v pračce?** _peh·reh seh toh fprahch·tseh_

Shoes

I'd like…	**Chtěl** _m_/**Chtěla** _f_ **bych…** _khtyehl/khtyeh·lah bihkh…_
high-heels	**boty na vysokých podpatcích** _boh·tih nah vih·soh·keekh poht·paht·tseekh_
flats	**boty bez podpatků** _boh·tih behs poht·paht·koo_
boots	**kotníčkové boty** _koht·neech·koh·veh boh·tih_
loafers	**mokasíny** _moh·kah·see·nih_
sandals	**sandály** _sahn·dah·lih_
shoes	**boty** _boh·tih_
slippers	**papuče** _pah·poo·cheh_
sneakers	**tenisky** _teh·nihs·kih_
In size…	**Ve velikosti…** _veh·veh·lih·kohs·tih…_

For Numbers, see page 175.

Sizes

small	**malé** _mah_·**leh**
medium	**střední** _strzhehd_·**neh**
large	**veliké** _veh_·**lih**·**keh**
extra large	**extra veliké** _ehks_·trah _veh_·**lih**·**keh**
petite	**pro štíhlé** proh _shtee_·hleh
plus size	**netypické velikosti** _neh_·tih·pihts·**keh** _veh_·**lih**·kohs·tih

Newsagent & Tobacconist

Do you sell English-language books/newspapers?	**Prodáváte anglické knihy/noviny?** _proh_·**dah**·vah·teh _ahn_·glihts·**keh** _knih_·hih/noh·vih·nih
I'd like…	**Chtěl** m/**Chtěla** f **bych…** khtyehl/_khtyeh_·lah bihkh…
candy [sweets]	**bonbóny** _bohn_·**boh**·nih
chewing gum	**žvýkačku** _zhvee_·kahch·koo
a chocolate bar	**čokoládu** _choh_·koh·**lah**·doo
a cigar	**doutník** _doht_·**neek**
a pack/carton of cigarettes	**krabičku/kartón cigaret** _krah_·bih·chkoo/_kahr_·tohn tsih·gah·reht
a lighter	**zapalovač** _zah_·pah·loh·vahch
a magazine	**časopis** _chah_·soh·pihs
matches	**zápalky** _zah_·pahl·kih
a newspaper	**noviny** _noh_·vih·nih
a pen	**propisku** _proh_·pis·koo
a postcard/ postcards	**pohlednici/pohlednice** _poh_·hled·nyi·tsi/_poh_·hled·nyi·tse
a road/town map of…	**mapu cest a dálnic/města…** _mah_·poo tsehst ah _dahl_·nihts/_myehs_·tah…
a stamp	**známka** _znahm_·kah
stamps	**známky** _znahm_·kyh

Photography

I'd like…camera.	**Chtěl** m/**Chtěla** f **bych…fotoaparát.** khtyehl/khtyeh·lah bihkh…foh·toh·ah·pah·raht
an automatic	**automatický** ow·toh·mah·tihts·kee
a digital	**digitální** dih·gih·tahl·nee
a disposable	**na jedno použití** nah·yehd·noh poh·oo·zhih·tee
I'd like…	**Chtěl** m/**Chtěla** f **bych…** khtyehl/khtyeh·lah bihkh…
a battery	**baterii** bah·teh·ryih
digital prints	**digitální printy** dih·gih·tahl·nee prihn·tih
a memory card	**paměťovou kartu** pah·myeh·t'oh·voh kahr·too
Can I print digital photos here?	**Můžu si tu vytisknout digitální fotky?** moo·zhoo sih too vih·tihsk·noht dih·gih·tahl·nee foht·kih

Souvenirs

Becher® brandy	**Becherovka®** beh·kheh·rohf·kah
bottle of wine	**láhev vína** lah·hehf vee·nah
box of chocolates	**bonboniéra** bohn·boh·nyeh·rah
calendar	**kalendář** kah·lehn·dahrzh
cut crystal	**broušené sklo** broh·sheh·neh skloh
Czech garnets	**České granáty** chehs·keh grah·nah·tih
doll	**panenka** pah·nehn·kah
hand-painted eggs	**velikonoční vajíčka** veh·lih·koh·noch·nee vah·yeech·kah
embroidery	**výšivky** vee·shihf·kih

Real treasures can be found at **jarmarki** (fairs): think Bohemian cut glass, handmade bells, embroidered tablecloths, folk costumes or plum brandy from a local distillery.

key ring	**přívěšek ke klíčům** _przhee_-vyeh-shehk _keh_-k_lee_-choom	
lace	**krajka** _krahy_-kah	
porcelain	**porcelán** _pohr_-tseh-_lahn_	
postcard	**pohlednica** _poh_-hlehd-nih-tsah	
pottery	**keramika** _keh_-rah-mih-kah	
puppet	**loutka** _loht_-kah	
scarf	**šátek** _shah_-tehk	
souvenir guide	**obrázkový průvodce** _ohb_-rahs-koh-_vee_ _proo_-voht-tseh	
tea towel	**utěrka** _oo_-tyehr-kah	
T-shirt	**tričko** _trihch_-koh	
wooden toys	**dřevěná hračka** _drzheh_-vyeh-_nah_ _hrahch_-kah	
Can I see this/that?	**Můžu to/tamto vidět?** _moo_-zhoo toh/_tahm_-toh _vih_-dyeht	
It's the one in the window/display case.	**To je ten z výlohy/výkladní skříně.** toh yeh tehn z _vee_-loh-hih/_veek_-lahd-nih _skrzee_-nyeh	
I'd like...	**Chtěl** m/**Chtěla** f **bych...** khtyehl/_khtyeh_-lah bihkh...	
a battery	**baterii** _bah_-teh-ryih	
a bracelet	**náramek** _nah_-rah-mehk	

a brooch	**brož** *brohzh*
earrings	**náušnice** <u>*nah*</u>*·oosh·nih·tseh*
a necklace	**náhrdelník** <u>*nah*</u>*·hrdehl·**neek***
a ring	**prsten** *prstehn*
a watch	**hodinky** <u>*hoh*</u>*·dihn·kih*
copper	**měď** *myehdy*
crystal	**křišťál** <u>*krzhih*</u>*·st'**ahl***
diamond	**diamant** <u>*dyah*</u>*·mahnt*
white/yellow gold	**bílé/žluté zlato** <u>*bee*</u>*·leh/*<u>*zhloo*</u>*·teh* <u>*zlah*</u>*·toh*
pearl	**perlu** <u>*pehr*</u>*·loo*
pewter	**cín** *ts**een***
platinum	**platina** <u>*plah*</u>*·tih·nah*
sterling silver	**stříbro** <u>*strzheeb*</u>*·roh*
Is this real?	**Je to pravé?** *yeh toh* <u>*prah*</u>*·veh*
Can you engrave it?	**Může se na tom rýt?** <u>*moo*</u>*·zheh seh na tohm r**eet***

ESSENTIAL

Where's the game?	**Kde se tady hraje?**	_gdeh_ seh _tah_•dih _hrah_•yeh
Where's…?	**Kde je…?**	_gdeh_ yeh…
the beach	**pláž**	p_lah_zh
the park	**park**	pahrk
the pool	**bazén**	bah•_zehn_
Is it safe to swim/ dive here?	**Dá se tady bezpečně plavat/skákat do vody?**	_dah_ seh _tah_•dih _behs_•pehch•nyeh _plah_•vaht/_skah_•kaht _doh_•voh•dih
Can I rent [hire] golf clubs?	**Můžu si vypůjčit golfové hole?**	_moo_•zhoo sih vih•_pooy_•chiht _gohl_•foh•veh _hoh_•leh
How much per hour?	**Kolik se platí za hodinu?**	_koh_•lihk seh _plah_•tee _zah_•hoh•dih•noo
How far is it to…?	**Jak je to daleko do…?**	_yahk_ yeh toh _dah_•leh•koh doh…
Can you show me on the map?	**Můžete mi to ukázat na mapě?**	_moo_•zheh•teh mih toh _oo_•kah•zaht nah•mah•pyeh

Watching Sport

When's…?	**Kdy se hraje…?**	_gdih_ seh _hrah_•yeh…
the basketball game	**basketbalový turnaj**	_bahs_•keht•bah•loh•_vee_ _toor_•nahy
the boxing match	**zápasy v boxu**	_zah_•pah•sih f_boh_•ksoo
the cycling race	**cyklistické závody**	_tsihk_•lihs•tihts•keh _zah_•voh•dih
the golf tournament	**golfový zápas**	_gohl_•foh•vee _zah_•pahs

the soccer [football] game	**fotbalové utkání** _foht_·bah·loh·veh _oot_·kah·nee
the tennis match	**tenisové utkání** _teh_·nih·soh·veh oot·kah·nee
the volleyball game	**volejbalová utkání** _voh_·lehy·bah·loh·vah _oot_·kah·nee
Which teams are playing?	**Které týmy hrají?** _kteh_·reh _tee_·mih _hrah_·yee
Where's…?	**Kde je…?** _gdeh_ yeh…
the horsetrack	**koňská dostihová dráha** _kohn's_·kah _doh_·stih·hoh·vah _drah_·hah

Czechs are ardent fans of **lední hokej** (ice hockey) and **fotbal** (soccer). Other popular sports include tennis, cycling, **kuželky** (bowling) and golf. Fitness centers are in abundance. During the winter, many Czechs enjoy downhill skiing and cross-country skiing, thanks to the number of winter sport resorts. These mountains also lend themselves to walking tours, hiking and mountain climbing (for registered climbers or climbing groups only).

Beskydy, **Jeseníky**, **Krkonoše** and **Šumava** are only four of numerous mountain ranges thriving with wintertime recreation. Snow lovers can enjoy well-kept and well-lit slopes as well as cross-country routes, sleighing routes and ever more modern ski lifts and equipment rentals. Skiing schools operate in almost all centers; there are also special slopes for children or snowboarders. Dedicated skaters can frequent winter stadiums (found in larger cities).

the racetrack	**závodní dráha** _zah_-vohd-nee _drah_-hah	
the stadium	**stadion** _stah_-dyohn	
Where can I place a bet?	**Kde mohu podat sázku?** _gdeh_ moh-hoo _poh_-daht **s**ahs-koo	

Playing Sport

Where's...?	**Kde je...?** _gdeh_ yeh...	
the golf course	**golfové hřiště** _gohl_-foh-**veh** hrzhihsh-tyeh	
the gym	**tělocvična** _tyeh_-lohts-fihch-nah	
the park	**park** pahrk	
the tennis court	**tenisový kurt** _teh_-nih-soh-**vee** koort	
How much per...?	**Kolik se platí za...?** _koh_-lihk seh _plah_-**tee** zah...	
day	**den** dehn	
hour	**hodinu** _hoh_-dih-noo	
game	**hru** hroo	
round	**kolo** koh-loh	
Can I rent [hire]...?	**Můžu si půjčit...?** _moo_-zhoo sih _pooy_-chiht...	
golf clubs	**golfové hole** _gohl_-foh-**veh** hoh-leh	
equipment	**vybavení** _vih_-bah-veh-nee	
a racket	**raketu** _rah_-keh-too	

At the Beach/Pool

Where's the beach/ pool?	**Kde je pláž/bazén?**	gdeh yeh plahzh/<u>bah</u>·zehn
Is there…?	**Je tu…?**	yeh too…
a kiddie [paddling] pool	**dětský bazén**	<u>dyehts</u>·kee <u>bah</u>·z**eh**n
an indoor/outdoor pool	**krytý/venkovní bazén**	<u>krih</u>·tee/<u>vehn</u>·kohv·nee <u>bah</u>·z**eh**n
a lifeguard	**plavčík**	<u>plahf</u>·cheek
Is it safe…here?	**Je tu bezpečně…?**	yeh too <u>behs</u>·pehch·nyeh…
to swim	**plavat**	<u>plah</u>·vaht
to dive	**skákat do vody**	<u>skah</u>·kaht doh voh·dih
for children	**pro děti**	<u>proh</u> dyeh·tih
I'd like to rent [hire]…	**Chtěl** m/**Chtěla** f **bych si půjčit…**	khtyehl/ khtyeh·lah <u>bihkh</u> sih p**oo**y·chiht…
a deck chair	**skládací lehátko**	<u>sklah</u>·dah·ts**ee** leh·<u>haht</u>·koh
diving equipment	**potápěčskou výstroj**	poh·<u>tah</u>·pyehchs·koh <u>vees</u>·trohy
a jet ski	**vodní skútr**	<u>vohd</u>·nee skootr
a motorboat	**motorový člun**	<u>moh</u>·toh·roh·vee chloon
a rowboat	**lodičku**	<u>loh</u>·dihch·koo
snorkeling equipment	**šnorchly**	<u>shnohr</u>·khlih
a surfboard	**surfingové prkno**	<u>sehr</u>·fihn·goh·veh prknoh
a towel	**ručník**	<u>rooch</u>·neek
an umbrella	**sluneční**	<u>sloo</u>·nehch·neek
water skis	**vodní lyže**	<u>vohd</u>·nee lih·zheh
a windsurfing board	**prkno na windsurfing**	prknoh nah <u>wind</u>·sur·fing
For…hours.	**Na…hodin.**	nah…<u>hoh</u>·dihn

For Numbers, see page 175.

Winter Sports

A lift pass for a day/ five days, please.	**Permanentku na vlek na den/na pět dní, prosím.** _pehr•mah•nehnt•koo nah•vlehk nah•dehn/nah•pyeht dnee proh•seem_
I want to rent [hire]…	**Chtěl m/Chtěla f bych si půjčit…** _khtyehl/ khtyeh•lah bihkh sih pooy•chiht…_
boots	**lyžařské boty** _lih•zhahrzh•skeh boh•tih_
a helmet	**přilbu** _przhihl•boo_
poles	**hole** _hoh•leh_
skis	**lyže** _lih•zheh_
a snowboard	**snowboardové prkno** _snoh•boh•ahr•doh•veh prknoh_
snowshoes	**sněžnice** _snyeh•zhnih•tseh_
These are too big/ small.	**Tyhle jsou moc velké/malé.** _tih•hleh ysoh mohts vehl•keh/mah•leh_
Are there lessons?	**Jsou tady cvičné louky?** _ysoh tah•dih tsfihch•neh loh•kih_
I'm a beginner.	**Jsem začátečník.** _Sem zah•chaa•tetch•nyeek_
I'm intermediate level.	**Jsem středně pokročilý/á.** _Sem strzed•nye poh•kroh•chil•lee/poh•kroh•chil•laah._

I'm experienced.	**Jsem pokročilý/á.** *Sem poh•kroh•chil•lee/ poh•kroh•chil•laah*
A trail [piste] map, please.	**Dejte mi mapu stezek, prosím.** *dehy•teh mih mah•poo steh•zehk proh•seem*

While in the Czech Republic, try to see at least one of the country's 12 UNESCO World Heritage sites: **Prague** Castle and the city's Old and New Towns; **Český Krumlov** (one of the largest palace complexes in Europe), **Telč** (Renaissance city houses); John of Nepomuk Church - an 18th century church in Zelená Hora; St Barnaby's cathedral (14th-16th century) in **Kutná Hora** and its old town; **Lednicko-Valtický** palace and park; folk Baroque architecture in the style of in **Holašovice**; the historical residence of the bishops and archbishops of Olomouc in **Kroměříž** - a castle surrounded by gardens; the16th century Renaissance castle in **Litomyšl**; the Baroque column of Holy Trinity in **Olomouc**; the Tugendhat villa (20th c) in **Brno**; and the St Prokop basilica and Jewish quarter in **Třebíč**.

YOU MAY SEE...

VLEKY	lifts
LYŽAŘSKÝ VLEK	drag lift
LANOVKA	cable car
SEDAČKOVÝ VLEK	chair lift
SNADNÁ STEZKA	novice
NÁROČNÁ STEZKA	intermediate
VELMI NÁROČNÁ STEZKA	expert
STEZKA ZAVŘENÁ/NEPŘÍSTUPNÁ	trail [piste] closed

Out in the Country

I'd like a map of…	**Chtěl** *m*/**Chtěla** *f* **bych mapu…**	khtyehl/khtyeh·lah bihkh mah·poo…
this region	**této oblasti**	teh·toh ohb·lahs·tih
walking routes	**turistických cest**	too·rihs·tihts·keekh tsehst
bike routes	**cyklistických stezek**	tsihk·lihs·tihts·keekh steh·zehk
the trails	**stezek**	steh·zehk
Is it easy/difficult?	**Je to snadné/náročné?**	yeh toh snahd·neh/ nah·roch·neh
Is it far/steep?	**Je to daleko/srázně?**	yeh toh dah·leh·koh/srahz·nyeh
How far is it to…?	**Jak je to daleko do…?**	yahk yeh toh dah·leh·koh doh…
Can you show me on the map?	**Můžete mi to ukázat na mapě?**	moo·zheh·teh mih toh oo·kah·zaht nah·mah·pee
I'm lost.	**Ztratil** *m*/**Ztratila** *f* **jsem se.**	strah·tihl/strah·tih·lah ysehm seh
Where is/are…?	**Kde je/jsou…?**	gdeh yeh/ysoh…
the bridge	**most**	mohst
the cave	**jeskyně**	yehs·kih·nyeh

the cliff	**útes**	_oo_·tehs
the forest	**les**	lehs
the lake	**jezero**	yeh·zeh·roh
the mountain	**hora**	hoh·rah
the nature reserve	**přírodní rezervace**	przhee·rohd·nee _nee·_reh·zehr·vah·tseh
the overlook	**vyhlídková terasa**	vih·hleed·koh·vah teh·rah·sah
the park	**park**	pahrk
the path	**pěšina**	pyeh·shih·nah
the picnic area	**místo na piknik**	mees·toh nah·pihk·nihk
the river	**řeka**	rzheh·kah
the sea	**moře**	moh·rzheh
the thermal springs	**termální zřídla**	tehr·mahl·nee zrzhee·dlah
the stream	**potok**	poh·tohk
the valley	**údolí**	oo·doh·lee
the vineyard	**vinice**	vih·nih·tseh
the waterfall	**vodopád**	voh·doh·pahd

ESSENTIAL

What is there to do in the evenings?	**Co se tady dá dělat večer?** *tsoh seh tah-dih dah dyeh-laht veh-chehr*
Do you have a program of events?	**Jaký je program?** *yah-kee yeh prohg-rahm*
What's playing at the movies tonight?	**Co dnes večer hrají v kině?** *tsoh dnehs veh-chehr hrah-yee fkih-nyeh*
Where's…?	**Kde je…?** *gdeh yeh…*
the downtown area	**centrum** *tsehn-troom*
the bar	**bar** *bahr*
the dance club	**diskotéka** *dihs-koh-teh-kah*
Is there an admission charge?	**Platí se tam vstupné?** *plah-tee seh tahm vstoop-neh*

Entertainment

Can you recommend…?	**Můžete mi doporučit…?** *moo-zheh-teh mih doh-poh-roo-chiht…*
a concert	**koncert** *kohn-tsehrt*
a movie	**film** *fihlm*
an opera	**operu** *oh-peh-roo*
a play	**představení** *przheht-stah-veh-nee*
When does it start/end?	**V kolik se začíná/končí?** *fkoh-lihk seh zah-chee-nah/kohn-chee*
I like…	**Mám moc rád *m*/rada *f*…** *mahm mohts raht/rah-dah…*

classical music	**klasickou hudbu** _klah_•sih•tskoh _hood_•boo
folk music	**lidovou hudbu** _lih_•doh•voh _hood_•boo
jazz	**džez** dzhehz
pop music	**pop** pohp
rap	**rap** rahp

For Tickets, see page 18.

Nightlife

What is there to do in the evenings?	**Co se tady dá dělat večer?** tsoh seh _tah_•dih d**ah** _dyeh_•laht _veh_•chehr
Can you recommend…?	**Můžete mi doporučit…?** _moo_•zheh•teh mih _doh_•poh•roo•chiht…
a bar	**bar** bahr
a casino	**kasino** _kah_•sih•noh
a dance club	**diskotéky** _dihs_•koh•teh•kih

YOU MAY HEAR…

Vypněte mobily, prosím. _vihp_•nyeh•teh _moh_•bih•lih _proh_•s**ee**m

Turn off your cell [mobile] phones, please.

a gay club	**klub pro homosexuály** *kloop proh hoh•moh•seh•ksoo•ah•lih*	
a nightclub	**noční klub** *nohch•nee kloop*	
Is there live music?	**Je tam živá hudba?** *yeh tahm zhih•vah hood•bah*	
How do I get there?	**Jak se tam dostanu?** *yahk seh tahm dohs•tah•noo*	
Is there an admission charge?	**Platí se tam vstupné?** *plah•tee seh tahm fstoop•neh*	
Let's go dancing.	**Pojďme si tančit.** *pohy•dymeh sih tahn•chiht*	
Is this area safe at night?	**Je to tu v noci bezpečné?** *Yeh toh too vno•tsi bez•petch•neh?*	

There are plenty of clubs to chose from in cities like Prague, Brno and Ostrava. Ostrava boasts an entire street with clubs, called **Stodolní**. The variety is wide – from dance to jazz and other music clubs – and hours are extensive (usually from early evening to early morning). It is advisable to have some ID such as a driver's license on you to get past the doorman.

Special Requirements

Business Travel

ESSENTIAL

I'm here on business.	**Jsem tady služebně.**	ysehm <u>tah</u>·dih <u>sloo</u>·zhehb·nyeh
Here's my business card.	**Zde je moje vizitka, prosím.**	zdeh yeh <u>moh</u>·yeh <u>vih</u>·ziht·kah proh·<u>seem</u>
Can I have your card?	**Můžu Vás poprosit o vaši vizitku?**	<u>moo</u>·zhoo vahs <u>poh</u>·proh·siht oh <u>vah</u>·shih <u>vih</u>·ziht·koo
I have a meeting with…	**Mám setkání s…**	mahm <u>seht</u>·kah·nee s…
Where's…?	**Kde je…?**	gdeh yeh…

the business center **byznysové centrum** <u>bihz</u>·nih·soh·veh <u>tsehn</u>·troom
the convention hall **konferenční sál** <u>kohn</u>·feh·rehnch·nee sahl
the meeting room **jednací síň** <u>yehd</u>·nah·tsee seen'

YOU MAY HEAR…

Máte domluvené setkání? <u>mah</u>·teh <u>doh</u>·mloo·veh·neh <u>seht</u>·kah·nee	Do you have an appointment?
S kým? skeem	With whom?
Je na schůzí. yeh nah <u>skhoo</u>·zee	He/She is in a meeting.
Okamžik, prosím. <u>oh</u>·kahm·zhihk proh·<u>seem</u>	One moment, please.
Posaďte se, prosím. <u>poh</u>·sahdy·teh seh proh·<u>seem</u>	Have a seat.
Dáte si něco k pití? <u>dah</u>·teh sih <u>nyeh</u>·tsoh <u>kpih</u>·tee	Would you like something to drink?
Děkuji za příchod. <u>dyeh</u>·koo·yih zah <u>przhee</u>·khohd	Thank you for coming.

On Business

I'm here to attend…	**Přijel** *m*/**Přijela** *f* **jsem na…** _przhih•yehl/_ _przhih•yeh•lah ysehm nah…_
a seminar	**seminář** _seh•mih•nahrzh_
a conference	**konferenci** _kohn•feh•rehn•tsih_
a meeting	**setkání** _seht•kah•nee_
My name is…	**Jmenuji se…** _ymeh•noo•yih seh…_
May I introduce my colleague…	**Dovolte, abych Vám představil svého kolegu…** _doh•vohl•teh ah•bih vahm przhehd•stah•vihl sveh•hoh koh•leh•goo…_

There are two ways of addressing people in Czech: the first, **Pane/Paní** (sir/madam) or **Vy** (formal you) is used with professionals, elderly people and those whom you do not know well; the informal **ty** (you) is used with young people, children and close acquaintances. Using first names in semi-formal contacts is acceptable only if the name is preceded by **Pane/Paní**.

I have a meeting/an appointment with…	**Mám setkání/Jsem domluvený s…** mahm <u>seht</u>•kah•nee/ysehm <u>dohm</u>•loo•veh•nee s…
I'm sorry I'm late.	**Promiňte, že jdu pozdě.** <u>proh</u>•mihn'•teh zheh ydoo <u>pohzh</u>•dyeh
I need an interpreter.	**Chtěl m/Chtěla f bych tlumočníka.** khtyehl/<u>khtyeh</u>•lah bihkh <u>tloo</u>•mohch•<u>nee</u>•kah
You can reach me at the…Hotel.	**Můžete mne najít v…Hotelu.** <u>moo</u>•zheh•teh mneh <u>nah</u>•yeet f…<u>hoh</u>•teh•loo
I'm here until…	**Zdržím se tady do…** <u>zdrzheem</u> seh tah•dih doh…
I need to…	**Potřebuji…** <u>poh</u>•trzheh•boo•yih…
make a call	**zavolat** <u>zah</u>•voh•laht
make a photocopy	**udělat xerokopie** <u>oo</u>•dyeh•laht <u>kseh</u>•roh•koh•pyeh
send an e-mail	**poslat e-mail** <u>pohs</u>•laht eh•mehyl
send a fax	**faxovat** <u>fah</u>•ksoh•vaht
send a package (overnight)	**poslat balík (přes noc)** <u>pohs</u>•laht <u>bah</u>•leek (przhehs nohts)
It was a pleasure to meet you.	**Těší mě.** <u>tyeh</u>•shee myeh

For Communications, see page 46.

Traveling with Children

ESSENTIAL

Is there a discount for children?	**Je na děti sleva?** *yeh <u>nah</u>•dyeh•tih <u>sleh</u>•vah*
Can you recommend a babysitter?	**Můžete mi doporučit opatrovnice?** *<u>moo</u>•zheh•teh mih <u>doh</u>•poh•roo•chiht <u>oh</u>•paht•rohv•nih•tseh*
Could we have a highchair/child's seat?	**Můžeme dostat židličku/židli pro dítě?** *<u>moo</u>•zheh•meh dohs•taht <u>zhih</u>•dlih•chkoo/<u>zhih</u>•dlih proh <u>dee</u>•tyeh*
Where can I change the baby?	**Kde mohu přebalit dítě?** *gdeh <u>moh</u>•hoo <u>przheh</u>•bah•liht <u>dee</u>•tyeh*

Out & About

Can you recommend something for the kids?	**Můžete mi doporučit někoho na hlídání děti?** *<u>moo</u>•zheh•teh mih <u>doh</u>•poh•roo•chiht <u>nyeh</u>•koh•hoh nah <u>hlee</u>•<u>dah</u>•nee <u>dyeh</u>•tih*

YOU MAY HEAR...

Jak je roztomilé! *yahk yeh rohz•toh•mih•leh* — How cute!
Jak se jmenuje? *yahk seh ymeh•noo•yeh* — What's his/her name?
Kolik je mu let? *koh•lihk yeh moo leht* — How old is he/she?

Where's...?	**Kde je...?** *gdeh yeh...*
the amusement park	**lunapark** *loo•nah•pahrk*
the arcade	**prostor s hracími automaty** *prohs•tohr shrah•tsee•mih ow•toh•mah•tih*
the kiddie [paddling] pool	**dětský bazén** *dyeht•skee bah•zehn*
the park	**park** *pahrk*
the playground	**dětské hřiště** *dyeht•skeh hrzhihsh•tyeh*
the zoo	**zoo** *zoh*
Are kids allowed?	**Děti mohou vstoupit?** *dyeh•tih moh•hoh fstoh•piht*
Is it safe for kids?	**Je to bezpečné pro děti?** *yeh toh behs•pehch•neh proh•dyeh•tih*
Is it suitable for... year olds?	**Je to vhodné pro...letý?** *yeh toh fhohd•neh proh...leh•tee*

For Numbers, see page 175.

Baby Essentials

Do you have...?	**Máte...?** *mah•teh...*
a baby bottle	**dětskou láhev s dudlíkem** *dyeht•skoh lah•hehf sdood•lee•kehm*
baby wipes	**navlhčené ubrousky** *nahvl•hcheh•neh oo•broh•skih*
a car seat	**autosedačku** *ow•toh•seh•dahch•koo*

a children's menu/ portion	**jídelník pro děti/dětskou porci** _yee_·dehl·neek proh _dyeh_·tih/_dyeht_·skoh _pohr_·tsih
a child's seat/ highchair	**židli pro dítě/židličku** _zhih_·dlih proh _dee_·tyeh/_zhih_·dlih·chkoo
a crib/cot	**kolébku/skládací postel** _koh_·lehp·koo/_sklah_·dah·ts**ee** pohs·tehl
diapers [nappies]	**plenky** _plehn_·kih
formula	**dětskou směs** _dyeht_·skoh smyehs
a pacifier [dummy]	**dudlík** _dood_·l**ee**k
a playpen	**ohrádku** _oh_·hrahd·koo
a stroller [pushchair]	**kočárek** _koh_·ch**ah**·rehk
Can I breastfeed the baby here?	**Můžu zde kojit dítě?** _moo_·zhoo zdeh _koh_·yiht _dee_·tyeh
Where can I change the baby?	**Kde mohu přebalit dětí?** gdeh _moh_·hoo _przheh_·bah·liht dyeh·t**ee**

For Dining with Children, see page 61.

Babysitting

Can you recommend a reliable babysitter?	**Můžete mi doporučit spolehlivou opatrovnice?**	_moo_•zheh•teh mih <u>doh</u>•poh•roo•chiht <u>spoh</u>•leh•hlih•voh <u>oh</u>•paht•rohv•nih•tseh
What's the charge?	**Kolik to stojí?**	<u>koh</u>•lihk toh <u>stoh</u>•yih
I'll/we'll be back at…	**Vrátím/vrátíme se…**	Vraatyeem/<u>Vraa</u>•tyee•meh seh…
I can be reached at…	**Můžete mě volat na číslo…**	_moo_•zheh•teh myeh <u>voh</u>•laht nah <u>chees</u>•loh…

For Time, see page 177.

Health & Emergency

Can you recommend a pediatrician?	**Můžete mi doporučit nějakého pediatru?**	_moo_•zheh•teh mih <u>doh</u>•poh•roo•chiht <u>nyeh</u>•yah•<u>keh</u>•hoh <u>peh</u>•dyaht•roo
My child is allergic to…	**Moje dítě má alergii na…**	<u>moh</u>•yeh <u>dee</u>•tyeh m**ah** <u>ah</u>•lehr•gyih nah…
My child is missing.	**Moje dítě se ztratilo.**	<u>moh</u>•yeh <u>dee</u>•tyeh seh <u>strah</u>•tih•loh
Have you seen a boy/girl?	**Neviděl jste chlapce/děvčátko?**	<u>neh</u>•vih•dyehl ysteh <u>khlahp</u>•tseh/<u>dyehf</u>•ch**ah**•tkoh

For Police, see page 155.

Disabled Travelers

ESSENTIAL

Is there…?	**Je zde…?** *yeh zdeh…*
access for the disabled	**přístup pro tělesně postižené** *przhee·stoop proh tyeh·lehs·nyeh pohs·tih·zheh·neh*
a wheelchair ramp	**podjezd pro invalidní vozíky** *pohd·yehzd proh ihn·vah·lihd·nee voh·zee·kih*
a handicapped-[disabled-] accessible toilet	**toalety pro tělesně postižené** *toh·ah·leh·tih proh tyeh·lehs·nyeh pohs·tih·zheh·neh*
I need…	**Potřebuji…** *poh·trzheh·boo·yih…*
assistance	**pomoc** *poh·mohts*
an elevator [lift]	**výtah** *vee·tah*
a ground-floor room	**pokoj v přízemí** *poh·kohy fprzee·zeh·mih*

Asking for Assistance

I'm disabled.	**Jsem tělesně postižený** *m*/**postižená** *f*. *ysehm tyeh·lehs·nyeh pohs·tih·zheh·nee/pohs·tih·zheh·nah*
I'm deaf.	**Jsem hluchý** *m*/**hluchá** *f*. *ysehm hloo·khee/hloo·khah*
I'm visually/hearing impaired.	**Špatně vidím/slyším.** *shpaht·nyeh vih·deem/slih·sheem*
Please speak louder.	**Prosím, mluvte hlasitěji.** *Proh·seem, mloof·teh hlah·sih·tye·yi*
I'm epileptic.	**Jsem epileptik.** *ysehm eh·pih·lep·tik*

I'm unable to walk far/use the stairs.	**Nemůžu moc chodit/používat schody.** *neh•moo•zhoo mohts khoh•diht/poh•oo•zhee•vaht skhoh•dih*
Can I bring my wheelchair?	**Můžu být na invalidním vozíku?** *moo•zhoo beet nah ihn•vah•leed•neem voh•zee•koo*
Are guide dogs permitted?	**Můžu přijít s mým psem-průvodcem?** *moo•zhoo przhih•yeet smeem psehm proo•vohd•tsehm*
Can you help me?	**Můžete mi pomoci?** *moo•zheh•teh mih poh•moh•tsih*
Please open/hold the door.	**Otevřte/Podržte dveře, prosím.** *oh•teh•vrzhteh/pohd•rzhteh dveh•rzheh proh•seem*

For Health, see page 158.

In an Emergency

Emergencies

ESSENTIAL

Help!	**Pomoc!** _poh_‑mohts
Go away!	**Jděte pryč!** _ydyeh_‑teh prihch
Stop, thief!	**Zastavte zloděje!** _zahs_‑tahf‑teh _zloh_‑dyeh‑yeh
Get a doctor!	**Zavolejte lékaře!** _zah_‑voh‑lehy‑teh _leh_‑kah‑rzheh
Fire!	**Hoří!** _hoh_‑rzh**ee**
I'm lost.	**Ztratil** m/**Ztratila** f **jsem se.** _strah_‑tihl/_strah_‑tih‑lah ysehm seh
Can you help me?	**Můžete mi pomoci?** _moo_‑zheh‑teh mih _poh_‑moh‑tsih

In an emergency, dial **112**.
You can also dial: **150** for the fire brigade, **155** for an ambulance, or **158** for the police.

Police

ESSENTIAL

Call the police!	**Zavolejte policii!** _zah_‑voh‑lehy‑teh _poh_‑lih‑tsyih
Where's the police station?	**Kde je policejní stanice?** _gdeh_ yeh _poh_‑lih‑tsehy‑n**ee** _stah_‑nih‑tseh
There's been an accident/attack.	**Došlo k této události/útoku.** _doh_‑shloh kt**eh**‑toh oo‑dah‑lohs‑tih/_oo_‑toh‑koo
My child is missing.	**Moje dítě se ztratilo.** _moh_‑yeh _dee_‑tyeh seh _strah_‑tih‑loh

I need...	**Potřebuji...** _poh_•trzheh•boo•yih...
an interpreter	**tlumočníka** _tloo_•mohch•nee•kah
to contact	**se spojit s mým právníkem** _seh_ spoh•yiht smeem
my lawyer	_prahv_•nee•kehm
to make	**zavolat** _zah_•voh•laht
a phone call	
I'm innocent.	**Jsem nevinný m/nevinná f.** ysehm _neh_•vihn•nee/
	neh•vihn•nah

YOU MAY HEAR...

Vyplňte prosím tento formulář.	Please fill out this form.
vihpl•n'teh _proh_•seem _tehn_•toh _fohr_•moo•lahrz	
Doklad totožnosti, prosím. _dohk_•lahd	Your ID, please.
toh•tohzh•nohs•tih _proh_•seem	
Kdy/Kde se to stalo? gdih/gdeh seh toh	When/Where did it
stah•loh	happen?
Jak on vypadal m/ona vypadala f?	What does he/she look
yahk on _vih_•pah•dahl/_oh_•nah _vih_•pah•dah•lah	like?

Crime & Lost Property

I want to report...	**Chtěl m/Chtěla f bych ohlásit...** khtyehl/_khtyeh_•lah
	bihkh _oh_•hlah•siht...
a mugging	**přepadení** _przheh_•pah•deh•nee
a rape	**znásilnění** _znah_•sihl•nyeh•nee
a theft	**krádež** _krah_•dehzh
I've been robbed/	**Okradli/přepadli mě.** _oh_•krahd•lih/_przheh_•pahd•lih
mugged.	myeh

156

I've lost my…	**Ztratil** m/**Ztratila** f **jsem…** _strah_·tihl/_strah_·tih·lah ysehm…
My…has been stolen.	**Ukradli mi…** _oo_·krahd·lih mih…
backpack	**batoh** _bah_·toh
bicycle	**kolo** _koh_·loh
camera	**fotoaparát** _foh_·toh·ah·pah·_raht_
cell [mobile] phone	**mobilní telefon** _moh_·bihl·nee teh·leh·fohn
(rental) car	**auto (z půjčovny)** _ow_·toh (_spooy_·chohv·nih)
computer	**počítač** _poh_·chee·tahch
credit card	**kreditní kartou** _kreh_·diht·nee _kahr_·toh
jewelry	**šperky** _shpehr_·kih
money	**peníze** _peh_·nee·zeh
passport	**pas** _pahs_
purse [handbag]	**kabelku** _kah_·behl·koo
travelers check [cheque]	**cestovní šeky** _tsehs_·tohv·nee shehk
wallet	**peněženku** _peh_·nyeh·zhehn·koo
I need a police report for my insurance.	**Potřebuji zprávu od policie pro pojišťovnu.** _poht_·rzheh·boo·yih _sprah_·voo _oht_·poh·lih·tsyeh _proh_·poh·yihsh·t'ohv·noo
Where is the British/ American/Irish embassy?	**Kde najdu britskou/americkou, irskou ambasádu?** _Kdeh_ _nay_·doo brits·koe/_ah_·meh·rits·koe _ahm_·bah·saa·doo?

157

Health

ESSENTIAL

I'm sick [ill].	**Jsem nemocný *m*/nemocná *f*.** ysehm neh·mohts·nee/neh·mohts·nah
I need an English-speaking doctor.	**Potřebuji lékaře, který mluví anglicky.** poht·rzheh·boo·yih leh·kah·rzheh kteh·ree mloo·vee ahn·glihts·kih
It hurts here.	**Tady to bolí.** tah·dih toh boh·lee
I have a stomachache.	**Bolí mí břicho.** boh·lee mee brzhih·khoh

Finding a Doctor

Can you recommend a doctor/dentist?	**Můžete mi doporučit lékaře/zubáře?** moo·zheh·teh mih doh·poh·roo·chiht leh·kah·rzheh/zoo·bah·rzheh
Could the doctor come to see me here?	**Mohl by mě lékař navštívit tady?** mohl bih myeh leh·kahrzh nahf·shtee·viht tah·dih
What are the office hours?	**V kolik přijímá?** fkoh·lihk przhih·yee·mah
Can I make an appointment...?	**Mohu se objednat termín...?** moh·hoo seh ohb·yehd·naht tehr·meen...
for today	**na dnešek** nah·dneh·shehk
for tomorrow	**na zítra** nah·zeet·rah
as soon as possible	**co nejdříve** tsoh nehy·drzhee·veh
It's urgent.	**Je to naléhavé.** yeh toh nah·leh·hah·veh

Symptoms

I'm bleeding.	**Jsem krvacení.** ysehm krfah·tseh·nee
I'm...	**Mám...** mahm...
constipated	**zácpu** zah·tspoo

dizzy	**závratě hlavy** <u>zah</u>·vrah·tyeh <u>hlah</u>·vih
nauseous	**nevolnosti** <u>neh</u>·vohl·nohs·tih
I'm vomiting.	**Zvracím.** <u>zvrah</u>·tseem
It hurts here.	**Tady to bolí.** <u>tah</u>·dih toh boh·<u>lee</u>
I have…	**Mám…** mahm…
an allergic reaction	**alergii** <u>ah</u>·lehr·gyih
a chest pain	**bolesti v hrudniku** <u>boh</u>·lehs·tih <u>fhrood</u>·nih·koo
cramps	**křeče** <u>krze</u>·tche
diarrhea	**průjem** <u>proo</u>·yem
an earache	**bolest ucha** <u>boh</u>·lehst oo·khah
a fever	**horečku** <u>hoh</u>·rehch·koo
pain	**bolesti** <u>boh</u>·lehs·tih
a rash	**vyrážku** <u>vih</u>·**rah**zh·koo
a sprain	**vyvrtnutí** <u>vih</u>·vrtnoo·tee
some swelling	**otok** <u>oh</u>·tohk
a sore throat	**bolesti v krku** <u>boh</u>·lehs·tih f kr·koo
a stomachache	**bolesti břicha** <u>boh</u>·lehs·tih <u>brzhih</u>·khah
sunstroke	**úpal** <u>oo</u>·pahl
I've been sick [ill]	**Jsem nemocný** *m*/**nemocná** *f* **již…dni.** ysehm
for…days.	<u>neh</u>·mohts·**nih**/<u>neh</u>·mohts·**nah** yihzh…dnih

For Numbers, see page 175.

Conditions

I'm... **Jsem...** *ysehm...*

anemic **anemik** *ah·neh·mihk*

asthmatic **astmatik** *ahst·mah·tihk*

diabetic **diabetik** *dyah·beh·tihk*

epileptic. **epileptik** *eh·pih·lep·tik*

YOU MAY HEAR...

Co se stalo? *tsoh seh stah·loh* — What's wrong?

Kde to bolí? *gdeh toh boh·lee* — Where does it hurt?

Bolí to tady? *boh·lee toh tah·dih* — Does it hurt here?

Užíváte nějaké jiné léky? *oo·zhee·vah·teh nyeh·yah·keh yih·neh leh·kih* — Are you taking any other medication?

Jste na něco alergický m/alergická f? *ysteh nah·nyeh·tsoh ah·lehr·gihts·kee/ ah·lehr·gihts·kah* — Are you allergic to anything?

Otevřete ústa. *oh·teh·frzheh·teh oo·stah* — Open your mouth.

Dýchejte zhluboka. *dee·hehy·teh shloo·boh·kah* — Breathe deeply.

Jdi do nemocnice. *ydih doh neh·mohts·nih·tseh* — Go to the hospital.

I'm allergic to antibiotics/penicillin. **Jsem alergický na antibiotika/penicillin.** *ysehm ah·lehr·gihts·kee nah ahn·tih·byoh·tih·kah/ peh·nih·tsih·lihn*

I have arthritis. **Mám artritida.** *mahm ahrt·rih·dih·tah*

I have high/low blood pressure. **Mám vysoký/nízký tlak.** *mahm vih·soh·kee/nihs·kee tlahk*

I have a heart condition.	**Mám srdeční potíže.** *mahm srdehch•nee poh•tee•zheh*
I'm on…	**Užívám…** *oo•zhih•vahm…*

Treatment

Do I need a prescription/medicine?	**Potřebuji recepty/léky?** *Pot•rzeh•boo•yi reh•tseh•ptih/leh•kih*
Can you prescribe a generic drug [unbranded medication]?	**Můžete mi předepsat generické léky?** *Moo•zheh•teh mih prze•deh•psaht ghe•neh•rits•keh leh•kih?*
Where can I get it?	**Kde to seženu?** *Kdeh toh seh•zheh•noo?*

For What to Take, see page 164.

Hospital

Notify my family.	**Uvědomte laskavě mou rodinu.** *oo•vyeh•dohm•teh lahs•kah•vyeh moh roh•dih•noo*
I'm in pain.	**Mám bolesti.** *mahm boh•lehs•tih*
I need a doctor/nurse.	**Potřebuji lékaře/zdravotní sestru.** *poht•rzeh•boo•yih leh•kah•rzheh/zdrah•voht•nee sehs•troo*

When are visiting hours?	**Kdy jsou návštěvní hodiny?** *gdih ysoh* <u>*nahf*</u>*-shtyehv-nee* <u>*hoh*</u>*-dih-nih*
I'm visiting…	**Jdu navštívit…** *ydoo* <u>*nahf*</u>*-shtee-viht…*

Dentist

I've broken a tooth.	**Udrobil se mi zub.** <u>*oo*</u>*-droh-bihl seh mih zoop*
I've lost a filling.	**Vypadla mi plomba.** *vih-pahd-lah mih* <u>*plohm*</u>*-bah*
I have a toothache.	**Bolí mě zub.** <u>*boh*</u>*-lee myeh zoop*
Can you fix this denture?	**Můžete mi opravit protézu?** <u>*moo*</u>*-zheh-teh mih* <u>*oh*</u>*-prah-viht* <u>*proh*</u>*-teh-zoo*

Gynecologist

I have menstrual cramps/a vaginal infection.	**Mám bolestivou menstruaci/vaginální infekci.** *mahm* <u>*boh*</u>*-lehs-tih-voh mehn-stroo-ah-tsih/* <u>*vah*</u>*-gih-nahl-nee ihn-fehk-tsih*
I missed my period.	**Menstruace se mi opožďuje.** *mehn-stroo-ah-tseh seh mih* <u>*oh*</u>*-pohzh-dyoo-yeh*
I'm on the pill.	**Beru antikoncepční pilulky.** <u>*beh*</u>*-roo* <u>*ahn*</u>*-tih-kohn-tsehp-chnee* <u>*pih*</u>*-lool-kih*
I'm not pregnant.	**Ne jsem těhotná.** *Neh ysehm* <u>*tyeh*</u>*-hoht-nah*

I'm (. . . months) pregnant.	**Jsem v (. . . měsíci) těhotenství.** *ysehm v (. . . mnyeh•sih•tsih) tyeh•hot•tenst•vee*
I haven't had my period for. . . months.	**Už...měsícú jsem neměla menstruace.** *oozh... myeh•see•tsoo ysehm neh•myeh•lah mehn•stroo•ah•tseh*

For Numbers, see page 175.

Optician

I've lost. . .	**Ztratil** *m***/Ztratila** *f* **jsem. . .** *strah•tihl/strah•tih•lah ysehm. . .*
a contact lens	**jednu kontaktní čočku** *yehd•noo kohn•tahkt•nee chohch•koo*
my glasses	**brýle** *bree•leh*
a lens	**čočky** *chohch•kih*

Payment & Insurance

How much?	**Kolik?** *koh•lihk*
Can I pay by credit card?	**Mohu zaplatit kreditní kartou?** *moh•hoo zah•plah•tiht kreh•diht•nee kahr•toh*
I have insurance.	**Mám pojištění.** *mahm poh•yihsh•tyeh•nee*
Can I have a receipt for my insurance?	**Mohu dostat stvrzenku pro pojišťovnu?** *moh•hoo dohs•taht stvrzehn•koo proh•poh•yihsh•ťohv•noo*

Pharmacies are marked with a green or white cross and the inscription **Lékarna**. They are generally open from Monday to Friday between 8 a.m. and 6 p.m., and on Saturday until noon. On the door of each pharmacy is a notice as to which pharmacy has extended hours. Not all pharmacies accept credit cards; it is therefore advisable to have cash handy.

Pharmacy

ESSENTIAL

Where's the nearest pharmacy [chemist's]?	**Kde je nejbližší lékárna?** _gdeh yeh <u>nehy</u>·blihzh·sh<u>ee</u> <u>leh</u>·**kahr**·nah_
What time does the pharmacy [chemist's] open/close?	**V kolik otvírají/zavírají lékárnu?** _<u>fkoh</u>·lihk <u>oht</u>·fee·rah·yee/<u>zah</u>·vee·rah·yee <u>leh</u>·**kahr**·noo_
What would you recommend for...?	**Jaký lék byste mi doporučil na...?** _yah·**kee** lehk bihs·teh mih <u>doh</u>·poh·roo·chihl nah..._
How much should I take?	**Kolik mám užívat?** _<u>koh</u>·lihk mahm <u>oo</u>·zh**ee**·vaht_
Can you fill [make up] this prescription for me?	**Můžete mi vydat léky na tento předpis?** _m<u>oo</u>·zheh·teh mih <u>vih</u>·daht <u>leh</u>·kih <u>nah</u>·tehn·toh <u>przheht</u>·pihs_
I'm allergic to...	**Mám alergii na...** _mahm <u>ah</u>·lehr·gyih nah..._

What to Take

How much should I take?	**Kolik mám užívat?** _<u>koh</u>·lihk mahm <u>oo</u>·zh**ee**·vaht_
How many times a day do I take it?	**Kolikrát denně to mám užívat?** _<u>koh</u>·lihk·**raht** dehn·hyeh toh mahm <u>oo</u>·zh**ee**·vaht_
Is it suitable for children?	**Je to vhodné pro děti?** _yeh toh <u>vhohd</u>·neh <u>proh</u>·dyeh·tih_
I'm taking...	**Beru...** _beh·roo..._
Are there side effects?	**Mají vedlejší účinki?** _<u>mah</u>·yee <u>vehd</u>·lehy·sh**ee** <u>oo</u>·chihn·kih_
I'd like some medicine for...	**Chtěl m/Chtěla f bych nějaký lék na...** _khtyehl/<u>khtyeh</u>·lah bihkh <u>nyeh</u>·yah·**kee** lehk nah..._
a cold	**rýmu** _<u>ree</u>·moo_

a cough	**kašel** _kah_·shehl
diarrhea	**průjem** _proo_·yehm
a headache	**bolesti hlavy** _boh_·les·tyi _hlah_·vy
insect bites	**štípance** _shtee_·pahn·tseh
motion [travel] sickness	**cestovní nemoc** _tsehs_·tohv·nee _neh_·mohts
a sore throat	**bolení v krku** _boh_·leh·nee fkrkoo
sunburn	**spálení sluncem** _spah_·leh·nee _sloon_·tsehm
a toothache	**bolesti zubů** _boh_·les·tyi _zoo_·boo
an upset stomach	**bolení břicha** _boh_·leh·nee _brzhih_·khah

Basic Supplies

I need (some)...	**Potřebuji (nějaký)...** _Pot_·rzeh·boo·yi (_nyeh_·yah·kee)...
acetaminophen [paracetamol]	**paracetamol** _pah_·rah·tseh·tah·mohl
antiseptic cream	**antiseptický krém** _ahn_·tih·sehp·tihts·**kee** krehm
aspirin	**aspirin** _ahs_·pih·rihn
Band-Aid [plasters]	**náplasti** _naah_·plahs·tyi

YOU MAY SEE...

JEDENKRÁT/TŘIKRÁT DENNĚ	once/three times a day
TABLETY	tablets
KAPKA	drop
TABLETY/PILULKY	tablets/pills
IŽIČKY	teaspoons
PŘED/PO/S JÍDLEM	before/after/with meals
NALAČNO	on an empty stomach
SPOLKNĚTE V CELKU	swallow whole
MŮŽE ZPŮSOBIT OSPALOST	may cause drowsiness
POUZE PRO VNĚJŠÍ POUŽITÍ	for external use
NEPOLYKAT	do not ingest

bandages	**obvazy** _oh_‑bvah‑zih	
a comb	**hřeben** _hrzheh_‑behn	
condoms	**kondomy** _kohn_‑dohm	
contact lens solution	**roztok na čočky** _rohs_‑tohk _nah_‑choh‑chkih	
deodorant	**deodorant** _deh_‑oh‑doh‑rahnt	
a hairbrush	**kartáč na vlasy** _kahr_‑**tah**ch _nah_‑vlah‑sih	
hair spray	**lak na vlasy** lahk _nah_‑vlah‑sih	
ibuprofen	**ibuprofén** _ih_‑boo‑proh‑**feh**n	
insect repellent	**repelent proti hmyzu** _reh_‑peh‑lehnt _proh_‑tih hmih‑zoo	
lotion [moisturizing cream]	**balzám [hydratační krém]** _bahl_‑zahm [_hid_‑rah‑tah‑chnyee]	
a nail file	**pilník na nehty** _pihl_‑neek nah _neh_‑htih	
a (disposable) razor	**(jednoúčelový) holicí strojek** (_yehd_‑noh‑**oo**‑cheh‑loh‑**vee**) _hoh_‑lih‑**tsee** _stroh_‑yehk	
razor blades	**žiletky** _zhih_‑leht‑kih	
sanitary napkins [pads]	**dámské vložky** _dah_m‑skeh _vlohsh_‑kih	
scissors	**nůžky** _noosh_‑kih	
shampoo/ conditioner	**šampon/kondicionér** shahm‑pohn/ _kohn_‑dih‑tsyoh‑**neh**r	
soap	**mýdlo** _meed_‑loh	
sunscreen	**krém na opalování** _krehm_ nah‑oh‑pah‑loh‑**vah**‑nee	
tampons	**tampony** _tahm_‑poh‑nih	
tissues	**papírové kapesníky** _pah_‑pee‑roh‑**veh** _kah_‑pehs‑nee‑kih	
toilet paper	**toaletní papír** _toh_‑ah‑leht‑nee _pah_‑peer	
a toothbrush	**kartáček na zuby** _kahr_‑**tah**‑chek _nah_‑zoo‑bih	
toothpaste	**zubní pastu** _zoob_‑nee _pahs_‑too	

For Baby Essentials, see page 149.

The Basics

Grammar

In Czech, there are two forms for you: **ty** (singular) and **vy** (plural). These are used when talking to relatives, close friends and children as well as among young people. When addressing someone in a formal situation, you should use the formal **Vy**.

Word Order

Word order in Czech is usually as in English, i.e., subject-verb-object. However, word order can be more flexible, because the word ending (case) indicates the role of each word in the sentence.

Example: **Jana dala knihu Karlovi.** = **Jana dala Karlovi knihu.**
Jana gave Karel a book.

There are three ways you can ask a question in Czech:

1. invert the subject and the verb

Example: **To je pan Novák.** This is Mr. Novák. **Je to pan Novák?** Is this Mr. Novák?

2. add a rising intonation to an affirmative statement

Example: **Pan Novák?** Mr. Novák?

3. use question words

kde (where, place), **kam** (where, direction), **kdy** (when), **kdo** (who), **co** (what)

Example: **Kde jsi?** Where are you?

Kam jdeš? Where are you going?

Kdy se vrátíš? When are you coming back?

Kdo to je? Who is it?

Co budeme dělat? What are we going to do?

Negation

To form a sentence in the negative, simply add **ne** (not) before the verb.
Example: **Mám lístek.** I have a ticket.
Nemám lístek. I don't have a ticket.

Regular Verbs

Czech verbs are conjugated based on person, number, tense and gender. The
infinitive of most Czech verbs ends in **-t**.
There are four regular conjugation patterns for Czech verbs. The following
present, past and future forms of the verbs **dělat** (to do), **vidět** (to see), **nést**
(to take) and **kupovat** (to buy) represent these four patterns.

DĚLAT (to do)		Present	Past	Future
I	**já**	děl**ám**	děl**al jsem** *m* děl**ala jsem** *f*	bud**u** dělat
you (sing., inf.)	**ty**	děl**áš**	děl**al jsi** *m* děl**ala jsi** *f*	bud**eš** dělat
he/she/it	**on/ ona/ ono**	děl**á**	děl**al** *m* děl**ala** *f* děl**alo** *(neuter)*	bud**e** dělat
we	**my**	děl**áme**	děl**ali jsme** *m* děl**aly jsme** *f*	bud**eme** dělat
you (pl./fml.)	**vy/Vy**	děl**áte**	děl**ali jste** *m* děl**aly jste** *f*	bud**ete** dělat
they	**oni/ ony/ ona**	děl**ají**	děl**ali** *m* děl**aly** *f* děl**ala** *(neuter)*	bud**ou** dělat

VIDĚT (to see)		Present	Past	Future
I	**já**	vid**ím**	vid**ěl jsem** *m* vid**ěla jsem** *f*	bud**u** vidět
you (sing., inf.)	**ty**	vid**íš**	vid**ěl jsi** *m* vid**ěla jsi** *f*	bud**eš** vidět
he/she/it	**on/** **ona/** **ono**	vid**í**	vid**ěl** *m* vid**ěla** *f* vid**ělo** *(neuter)*	bud**e** vidět
we	**my**	vid**íme**	vid**ěli jsme** *m* vid**ěly jsme** *f*	bud**eme** vidět
you (pl./fml.)	**vy/Vy**	vid**íte**	vid**ěli jste** *m* vid**ěly jste** *f*	bud**ete** vidět
they	**oni/** **ony/** **ona**	vid**í**	vid**ěli** *m* vid**ěly** *f* vid**ěla** *(neuter)*	bud**ou** vidět

NÉST (to take)		Present	Past	Future
I	**já**	nes**u**	nesl **jsem** *m* nesla **jsem** *f*	bud**u** nést
you (sing., inf.)	**ty**	nes**eš**	nesl **jsi** *m* nesla **jsi** *f*	bud**eš** nést
he/she/it	**on/** **ona/** **ono**	nes**e**	nesl *m* nesla *f* nesl**o** *(neuter)*	bud**e** nést
we	**my**	nes**eme**	nesl**i jsme** *m* nesl**y jsme** *f*	bud**eme** nést
you (pl./fml.)	**vy/Vy**	nes**ete**	nesl**i jste** *m* nesl**y jste** *f*	bud**ete** nést
they	**oni/** **ony/** **ona**	nes**ou**	nesl**i** *m* nesl**y** *f* nesl**a** *(neuter)*	bud**ou** nést

KUPOVAT (to buy)		Present	Past	Future
I	**já**	kupuj**i**	kupoval **jsem** *m* kupovala **jsem** *f*	bud**u** kupovat
you (sing., inf.)	**ty**	kupuj**eš**	kupoval **jsi** *m* kupovala **jsi** *f*	bud**eš** kupovat
he/she/it	**on/ ona/ ono**	kupuj**e**	kupoval *m* kupoval**a** *f* kupoval**o** *(neuter)*	bud**e** kupovat
we	**my**	kupuj**eme**	kupoval**i jsme** *m* kupoval**y jsme** *f*	bud**eme** kupovat
you (pl./fml.)	**vy/Vy**	kupuj**ete**	kupoval**i jste** *m* kupoval**y jste** *f*	bud**ete** kupovat
they	**oni/ ony/ ona**	kupuj**í**	kupoval**i** *m* kupoval**y** *f* kupoval**a** *(neuter)*	bud**ou** kupovat

Irregular Verbs

Irregular verbs do not follow the normal rules and must be memorized. Here are two common irregular verbs, **być** (to be) and **iść** (to go):

BYĆ (to be)		Present	Past	Future
I	**já**	jsem	byl jsem *m* byla jsem *f*	budu
you (sing., inf.)	**ty**	jsi	byl jsi *m* byla jsi *f*	budeš
he/she/it	**on/ ona/ ono**	je	byl *m* byla *f* bylo *(neuter)*	bude
we	**my**	jsme	byli jsme *m* byly jsme *f*	budeme
you (pl./fml.)	**vy/Vy**	jste	byli jste *m* byly jste *f*	budete

they	oni/	jsou	byli *m*	budou
	ony/		byly *f*	
	ona		byla *(neuter)*	

JÍT (to go)		Present	Past	Future
I	**já**	jdu	šel jsem *m*	budu jít
			šla jsem *f*	
you (sing., inf.)	**ty**	jdeš	šel jsi *m*	budeš jít
			šla jsi *f*	
he/she/it	**on/**	jde	šel *m*	bude jít
	ona/		šla *f*	
	ono		šlo *(neuter)*	
we	**my**	jdeme	šli jsme *m*	budeme jít
			šly jsme *f*	
you (pl./fml.)	**vy/Vy**	jdete	šli jste *m*	budete jít
			šly jste *f*	
they	**oni/**	jdou	šli *m*	budou jít
	ony/		šly *f*	
	ona		šla *(neuter)*	

Nouns

Nouns in Czech are either masculine, feminine or neuter.

Masculine nouns usually end in a consonant (**student**, student; **muž**, man). A few of them have the ending **-a** (**kolega**, friend; **turista**, tourist).

Feminine nouns usually end in **-a** (žena, woman), **-e** (růže, rose) or a consonant (**radost**, joy; **povodeň**, flood).

Neuter nouns end in **-o** (**město**, city), **-í** (**náměstí**, town square) or **-e** (**pole**, field). Most plural masculine and feminine nouns end in **-i** or in **-y**, respectively; most neuter nouns end with **-a** in the plural.

The endings of nouns vary according to their role in the sentence. There are seven different cases (roles) in both the singular and plural.

There are **no articles** (a, an, the) in Czech.

Imperatives

Imperative sentences are formed by adding the appropriate ending to the verb stem.

Example: Go!

you go	ty	**Jdi!**
he/she/it goes	on *m*	**Ať jde!**
	ona *f*	
	ono *(neuter)*	
we go	my	**Jděme!**
you (pl./fml.) go	vy/Vy	**Jděte!**
they go	oni *m*	**Ať jdou!**
	ony *f*	
	ona *(neuter)*	

Adjectives

There are two groups of adjectives: strong and weak. Strong adjectives end in hard consonants or vowels **-ý** *m*, **-á** *f*, **-é** *(neuter)*. Soft adjectives end in soft consonants or í in the nominative (subject) case.

Adjectives must agree in gender, number and case with the nouns they modify.

	strong adjective		weak adjective	
masculine	**český**	Czech	**moderní**	modern
	student	student	**dům**	house
feminine	**česká**	Czech	**moderní**	modern
	žena	woman	**škola**	school
neuter	**české**	Czech	**moderní**	modern
	město	city	**auto**	car

Comparative & Superlative

The comparative is constructed by adding **-ejší, -ější** to adjectives ending in **-ský, -lý, -pý, -vý, -ný, -tý, -rý**, and the ending **-ší** to adjectives ending in **-bý, -dý, -hý, -chý, -ký, -oký, -eký**. The superlative is formed by adding **nej-** to the comparative.

Example:

levný (cheap)	**levnější** (cheaper)	**nejlevnější** (cheapest)
slabý (weak)	**slabší** (weaker)	**nejslabší** (weakest)

Pronouns

Pronouns, like nouns, decline according to gender, number and case. Personal pronouns (I, you, he, she, etc.) can look very different from their base forms according to what "role" they play in the sentence.

I	**já**
you (sing., inf.)	**ty**
he, she, it	**on/ona/ono**
we	**my**
you (pl./fml.)	**vy/Vy**
they	**oni** *m*/**ony** *f*/**ona** *(neuter)*

Possessive Adjectives

	masculine	feminine	neuter
my	**můj**	**moje**	**moje**
your (sing.)	**tvůj**	**tvoje**	**tvoje**
his/her	**jeho**	**jeho**	**jeho**
its	**její**	**její**	**její**
our	**náš**	**naše**	**naše**
your (pl.)	**váš**	**vaše**	**vaše**
their	**jejich**	**jejich**	**jejich**

Example:

To je můj dům. This is my house.
To je moje kniha. This is my book.
To je moje dítě. This is my child.

Adverbs

Most adverbs are derived from the corresponding adjectives by means of special suffixes:

adjectives	adverbs
1. **-ý**	**-e**
rychlý (fast)	**rychle**
2. **-ý**	**-ě**
špatný (bad)	**špatně**
3. **-ský, -zký, -cký**	**-sky, -zky, -cky**
český (Czech)	**česky**
hezký (pretty)	**hezky**
4. **-ý**	**-o**
chladný (cool)	**chladno**

ESSENTIAL

0	**nula** _noo_·lah
1	**jedna** _yehd_·nah
2	**dva** dvah
3	**tři** trzhih
4	**čtyři** _chtih_·rzhih
5	**pět** pyeht
6	**šest** shehst
7	**sedm** sehdm
8	**osm** ohsm
9	**devět** _deh_·vyeht
10	**deset** _deh_·seht
11	**jedenáct** _yeh_·deh·_nahtst
12	**dvanáct** _dvah_·nahtst
13	**třináct** _trzhih_·nahtst
14	**čtrnáct** chtrnahtst
15	**patnáct** _paht_·nahtst
16	**šestnáct** _shehst_·nahtst
17	**sedmnáct** _sehdm_·nahtst
18	**osmnáct** _ohsm_·nahtst
19	**devatenáct** _deh_·vah·teh·_nahtst
20	**dvacet** _dvah_·tseht
21	**dvacet jedna** _dvah_·tseht yehd·nah
22	**dvacet dva** _dvah_·tseht dvah
30	**třicet** _trzhih_·tseht
31	**třicet jedna** _trzhih_·tseht yehd·nah
40	**čtyřicet** _chtih_·rzhih·tseht

50	**padesát** _pah_·deh·**saht**
60	**šedesát** _sheh_·deh·**saht**
70	**sedmdesát** _sehdm_·deh·**saht**
80	**osmdesát** _ohsm_·deh·**saht**
90	**devadesát** _deh_·vah·deh·**saht**
100	**sto** _stoh_
101	**sto jedna** _stoh_ yehd·nah
200	**dvě stě** _dvyeh_ styeh
500	**pět set** _pyeht_ seht
1,000	**tisíc** _tih_·seets
10,000	**deset tisíc** _deh_·seht tih·**seets**
1,000,000	**milión** _mih_·lih·**ohn**

Ordinal Numbers

first	**první** prvnee
second	**druhý** _droo_·hee
third	**třetí** _trzheh_·tee
fourth	**čtvrtý** chtfrtee
fifth	**pátý** _pah_·tee
once	**jednou** _yehd_·noh
twice	**dvakrát** _dvahk_·raht
three times	**třikrát** _trzhihk_·raht

Czechs use the 24-hour clock when writing time, especially in schedules. Morning hours from 1:00 to noon are the same as in English. After noon, 12 should be added to the time: 1 p.m. is 13:00, 6 p.m. is 18:00, etc.

Time

ESSENTIAL

What time is it?	**Kolik je hodin?** _koh_·lihk yeh _hoh_·dihn
It's noon [midday].	**Je dvanáct hodin poledne.** yeh _dvah_·**naht**st _hoh_·dihn poh·**lehd**·neh
It's midnight.	**Je půlnoc.** yeh _pool_·nohts
From 9 o'clock to 5 o'clock.	**Od deváté do páté.** _ohd_·deh·**vah**·teh _doh_·**pah**·teh
twenty after [past] four	**za deset minut půl páté** _zah_·deh·seht mih·noot _pool_ pah·teh
a quarter to nine	**tři čtvrtě na devět** trzhih _chtvur_·tyeh _nah_·deh·vyeht
5:30 a.m./p.m.	**půl šesté/sedmnáct třicet** _pool_ _shehs_·teh/ _sehdm_·**nah**tst _tzhih_·tseht

Days

ESSENTIAL

Monday	**pondělí** _pohn_·dyeh·**lee**
Tuesday	**úterý** _oo_·teh·**ree**
Wednesday	**středa** _strzheh_·dah
Thursday	**čtvrtek** chtfrtehk
Friday	**pátek** _pah_·tehk
Saturday	**sobota** _soh_·boh·tah
Sunday	**neděle** _neh_·dyeh·leh

Dates

yesterday	**včera** _fcheh_•rah
today	**dnes** dnehs
tomorrow	**zítra** _zeet_•rah
day	**den** dehn
week	**týden** _tee_•dehn
month	**měsíc** _myeh_•seets
year	**rok** rohk
Happy Birthday	**Všechno nejlepší k narozenínám!**
	Vsheh•khnoh _ney_•lep•shee k _nah_•roh•zeh•nyih•nahm
Happy New Year	**Šťastný nový rok!** _Shtya_•stnee _noh_•vee rock

Months

January	**leden** _leh_•dehn
February	**únor** _oo_•nohr
March	**březen** _brzheh_•zehn
April	**duben** _doo_•behn
May	**květen** _kfyeh_•tehn
June	**červen** _chehr_•vehn
July	**červenec** _chehr_•veh•nets
August	**srpen** srpehn
September	**září** _zah_•rzhee

October	**říjen** <u>rzhee</u>•yehn
November	**listopad** <u>lih</u>•stoh•paht
December	**prosinec** proh•sih•nehts

Seasons

spring	**jaro** <u>yah</u>•roh
summer	**léto** <u>leh</u>•toh
fall [autumn]	**podzim** <u>pohd</u>•zihm
winter	**zima** <u>zih</u>•mah

Holidays

January 1	**Nový Rok, Den vzniku samostatného** New Year's Day, Czech Independence Day
March/April (movable)	**Velikonoce** Easter
May 1	**Svátek práce** Labor Day
May 8	**Den osvobození od fašismu** Victory over Fascism (Liberation Day)
July 5	**Den slovanských věrozvěstů Cyrila a Metoděje** Day of the Slavic Apostles Cyril and Methodius
July 6	**Mistr Jan Hus** Jan Hus Day
November 17	**Dne boje za svobodu a demokracii** Freedom and Democracy Day
December 25	**Sváty vánoční** Christmas Day
December 26	**svätého Štefana** Feast of St. Stephen

Main public holidays in the Czech Republic are connected with recent historical events, such as the liberation after World War II or the restoration of the Czech Republic after the break from Slovakia. Czechs usually spend holidays with their families and friends, enjoying leisure time in town or the countryside.

Conversion Tables

When you know	Multiply by	To find
ounces	28.3	grams
pounds	0.45	kilograms
inches	2.54	centimeters
feet	0.3	meters
miles	1.61	kilometers
square inches	6.45	sq. centimeters
square feet	0.09	sq. meters
square miles	2.59	sq. kilometers
pints (U.S./Brit)	0.47/0.56	liters
gallons (U.S./Brit)	3.8/4.5	liters
Fahrenheit	5/9, after 32	Centigrade
Centigrade	9/5, then +32	Fahrenheit

Kilometers to Miles Conversions

1 km	0.62 miles
5 km	3.1 miles
10 km	6.2 miles
50 km	31 miles
100 km	62 miles

Measurement

1 gram	**gram** *grahm*	= 0.035 oz.
1 kilogram (kg)	**kilo** *kee·loh*	= 2.2 lb
1 liter (l)	**liter** *leetr*	= 1.06 U.S./0.88 Brit. quarts
1 centimeter (cm)	**decimeter** *tsehn·tyh·mehtr*	= 0.4 inch
1 meter (m)	**meter** *mehtr*	= 3.28 feet
1 kilometer (km)	**kilometer** *kee·loh·mehtr*	= 0.62 mile

Temperature

-40° C – -40° F	-1° C – 30° F	20° C – 68° F
-30° C – -22° F	0° C – 32° F	25° C – 77° F
-20° C – -4° F	5° C – 41° F	30° C – 86° F
-10° C – 14° F	10° C – 50° F	35° C – 95° F
-5° C – 23° F	15° C – 59° F	

Oven Temperature

100° C – 212° F	177° C – 350° F
121° C – 250° F	204° C – 400° F
149° C – 300° F	260° C – 500° F

Dictionary

A

athletics atletika
ATM bankomat
attack útok
attractive přitažlivý
audio guide audio průvodce
aunt teta
Australia Austrálie
authentic pravý
authenticity pravost
available (free) volný

B

baby dítě
baby bottle dětská láhev
baby food kojenecká výživa
baby wipe navlhčené ubrousek
babysitter paní na hlídání děti
back (head) vzadu; **(body)** záda
backache bolest zad
backpack ruksak
bad špatný
bag kabelka
baggage [BE] zavazadlo
baggage reclaim [BE] výdej zavazadel
bakery pekařství
balcony balkón
ball míč
ballet balet
band (musical group) skupina
bandage obinadlo

bank banka
bar bar
barber holičství
basement suterén
basket košík
basketball košíková
bath *n* vana; *v* koupat
bathroom koupelna; **(toilet)** záchod
battery baterie; **(car)** akumulátor
battle site bitevní pole
be být
beach pláž
beam (headlight) světlo
beautiful krásný
because protože
bed postel
bedding přikrývky a povlečení
bedroom ložnice
before (time) před
begin začít
beginner začátečník
behind za
belong náležet
belt pásek
berth lůžko
between (time) mezi
bib bryndáček
bicycle jízdní kolo
bicycle route cyklistická stezka
big velký
bikini bikiny

adj adjective	**BE** British English	**prep** preposition
adv adverb	**n** noun	**v** verb

bill (restaurant) účet
binoculars dalekohled
bird pták
birthday narozeniny
bite (insect) štípnutí
bitter hořký
bizarre prapodivný
bladder močový měchýř
blanket přikrývka
bleach odbarvovací prostředek
bleed krvácet
blind roleta
blister puchýř
blocked ucpaný
blood krev
blood pressure krevní tlak
blouse blůza
blow dry vyfoukat
blue modrý
board *n* palubní
boarding card palubní vstupenka
boat trip výlet lodí
boil *n* **(ailment)** vřídek; *v* vařit
boiler kotel
bone kost
book kniha
bookstore knihkupectví
boots boty
boring nudný
born narodit se
borrow půjčit
botanical garden botanická zahrada
bottle láhev
bottle opener otvírač na láhve
bowel střevo
bowl miska
box krabička
boy chlapec
boyfriend milenec

bra podprsenka
bracelet náramek
brakes (bicycle, car) brzdy
break *v* rozbít
breakdown porucha
breast prso
breastfeed kojit
breathe dýchat
bridge most
bring přivést
British britský
brochure brožura
broken (damaged) rozbitý;
    (body part) zlomený
brooch brož
brother bratr
browse dívat se
bruise modřina
bucket kyblík
building budova
bulletin board nástěnka
burn *n* popálenina
bus autobus
bus station autobusové nádraží
bus stop autobusová zastávka
business class obchodní třída
busy něco mít
but ale
butane gas plyn
butcher řezník
button knoflík
buy koupit
by (near) u; **(time)** do
bye nashledanou

C

cafe kavárna
calendar kalendář
call (shout) přijít; **(telephone)** zavolat

camera fotoaparát
camp v tábořit
campsite kempink
can opener otvírač na plechovky
Canada Kanada
canal kanál
cancel zrušit
cancer (disease) rakovina
cap (clothing) čepice;
  (dental) korunka
car auto; **(train)** vagón
car park [BE] parkoviště
car rental půjčovna aut
carafe džbánek
card karta
careful opatrný
carpet koberec
cart vozík
case (suitcase) zavazadlo
cash n **(money)** hotovost; v proplatit;
  (exchange) vyměnit
casino kasino
castle hrad
cathedral katedrála
cave jeskyně
CD cédéčko
cell phone mobilní telefon
cemetery hřbitov
center of town centrum
ceramics keramika
certificate osvědčení
chain (necklace) řetízek
change n **(coins)** drobné; v
  (money) vyměnit; **(transportation)**
  přestoupit; **(reservation)** změnit;
  (a baby) přebalit dítě
changing facilities prostor
  na přebalování
charcoal dřevěné uhlí

charter flight speciál
cheap levný
check n šek; v kontrolovat
check in (hotel) ubytovat se
check out (hotel) uvolnit pokoj
cheers na zdraví
chemist [BE] lékárna
cheque [BE] šek
chess šachy
chest (body) prsa
child dítě
child's cot [BE] dětská postýlka
child's seat dětská sedačka
church kostel
cigar doutník
cigarette cigareta
cinema [BE] kino
claim check (luggage) zavazadlový
  lístek
clean adj čistý; v vyčistit
cliff útes
cling film [BE] potravinová fólie
clinic zdravotní středisko
clock hodiny
close adv **(near)** blízko; v zavírat
clothing store oděvy
cloudy oblačný
club (golf) golfová hůl
coast pobřeží
coat kabát
coat hanger ramínko
coatroom šatna
cockroach šváb
code (phone) směrovací číslo
coin mince
cold adj studený;
  (weather) chladný; n chlad
collect vyzvednout
color barva

comb hřeben
come přijít
comfortable pohodlný
commission provize
company (business) firma;
    (companionship) společnost
computer počítač
concert koncert
concert hall koncertní síň
concession sleva
concussion otřes mozku
conditioner (hair) kondicionér
condom kondom
conductor dirigent
confirm (reservation) potvrdit
connection (train) spojení
conscious vědomí
constant nepřetržitý
constipation zácpa
consulate konzulát
consult jít
contact v spojit se
contact lens kontaktní čočka
contagious nakažlivý
contain obsahovat
contraceptive antikoncepce
cook n **(chef)** kuchař; v vařit
cooker [BE] (appliance) vařič
cooking facilities kuchyňské vybavení
copper měď
copy kopie
corkscrew vývrtka
correct správný
cosmetics kosmetika
cost n cena; v stát
cottage chata
cotton bavlna
cough n kašel; v kašlat
country (nation) země

course (track, path) cesta;
    (medication) dávka
cover charge kuvert
cramps křeče
credit card kreditní karta
credit card number číslo kreditní karty
crib kolébka
crockery [BE] nádobí
crown (dental) korunka;
    (royal) koruna
cruise n zábavní plavba
crystal křišťál
cup šálek
currency měna
currency exchange office směnárna
customs celní prohlídka
cut (hair) ostřihat
cut glass broušené sklo
cutlery příbory
cycle route cyklistická stezka
cycling cyklistika
Czech adj český; n Czech
Czech Republic Česká Republika

D

delay zpoždění
delicatessen lahůdky
delicious chutný
deliver doručit
denim džínsovina
dental floss vlákno na čištění
    mezizubních prostorů
dentist zubař
denture protéza
deodorant deodorant
depart (train, bus) odjíždět;
    (plane) odlétat
department store obchodní dům
departure lounge odjezdová hala

deposit záloha
describe popsat
details podrobnosti
detergent prášek na praní
develop (photos) vyvolat
diabetic diabetik
diamond diamant
diaper plenka
diarrhea průjem
dice kostky
dictionary slovník
diesel (fuel) nafta;
   (vehicle) dieselový motor
diet dieta
difficult těžký
digital camera digitální fotoaparát
dining car jídelní vůz
dining room jídelna
dinner večeře
direct (train, flight) přímý
direction směr
directory (telephone) telefonní
   seznam
dirty špinavý
disabled *adj* tělesně postižený;
   n invalida
discount sleva
dish (meal) jídlo;
   (tableware) nádoba
dishcloth hadr na nádobí
dishwashing liquid prostředek
   na mytí nádobí
display window vitrína
disposable camera fotoaparát
   na jedno použití
dive skákat do vody
divorced rozvedený
dizzy závrativý
doctor doktor

doll panenka
dollar (U.S.) dolar
door dveře
double bed manželská postel
downtown centrum města
dozen tucet
dress šaty
drink *n* pití; *v* pít
drive jet
driver řidič
driver's license řidičský průkaz
drowning topit se
drugstore drogerie
dry clean *v* chemicky
   vyčistit
dry cleaner čistírna
dubbed dabovaný
dummy [BE] dudlík
during během
dustbin [BE] popelnica
duvet peřina
ear ucho

E

ear drops kapky do uší
early brzo
earring náušnice
east východ
easy snadný
eat jíst
economy class ekonomická
   třída
elastic *adj* elastický
electric razor elektrický holicí
   strojek
electrical outlet elektrické
   zásuvka
electronic elektronický
elevator výtah

e-mail elektronická pošta
e-mail address emailová adresa
embassy velvyslanectví
emerald smaragd
emergency *adj* naléhavý
emergency exit nouzový východ
empty prázdný
enamel email
end končit
engaged zasnoubený
engine motor
engineering strojírenství
England Anglie
English *adj* anglický;
　(language) angličtina;
　n Anglik
enjoy mít rád
enlarge zvětšit
enough dost
entertainment guide kulturní
　přehled
entrance fee vstupné
entry visa vstupní vízum
envelope obálka
epileptic *n* epileptik
equipment (sports) vybavení
error chyba
escalator eskalátor
essential nezbytný
e-ticket elektronický lístek
evening večer
every každý
examination (medical) vyšetření
example příklad
except kromě
excess luggage nadváha
excursion výlet
exhausted vyčerpaný
exchange *v* vyměnit

exchange rate kurz
exit *n* východ; **(highway)** sjezd
expensive drahý
exposure (photos) snímek
express spěšně
extension linka
extract (tooth) vytrhnout

F

fabric látka
face obličej
facial ošetřit obličej
facility zručnost
factor (sunscreen) faktor
family rodina
famous známý
fan (ventilation) větrák
far daleko sighted
farm statek
far-sighted dalekozraký
fast (clock) rychlý napřed
fast-food restaurant rychlé
　občerstvení
father otec
faucet kohoutek
faulty vadné
favorite oblíbený
fax fax
feed nakojit
feel cítit
female *adj* ženská; *n* žena
fever horečka
few málo
field pole
fight (brawl) rvačka
fill vyplnit
filling (dental) plomba
film (movie) film; **(camera)** film
filter filtr

find najít
fine (well) dobře; **(penalty)** pokuta
finger prst
fire krb; **(disaster)** požár
fire alarm požární hlásič
fire brigade [BE] hasiči
fire department hasiči
fire exit nouzový východ
fire extinguisher hasicí přístroj
first class první třída
fit (clothes) slušet
fitting room zkušební kabina
fix spravit
flashlight ruční
flat (puncture) píchlý
flavor příchuť
flea blecha
flight letadlo
flight number let číslo
floor (level) poschodí
florist květiny
flower květ
flu (influenza) chřipka
fly (insect) moucha
foggy mlhavo
food jídlo
food poisoning otrava
   potravinami
foot chodidlo
football [BE] fotbal
footpath pěšina
for (time) na; **(towards)** do
foreign currency zahraniční měna
forest les
forget zapomenout
fork vidlička
form formulář
formal dress formální oblečení
fortunately naštěstí

fountain kašna
foyer (hotel, theater) foyer
fracture zlomenina
frame (glasses) obroučky
free (available) volný;
   (no charge) zadarmo
freezer mraznička
frequent často
fresh čerstvý
friend přítel
friendly přátelský
frightened vystrašený
from (place) z; **(time)** od
front *adj* přední;
   (head) vpředu
frost mráz
frying pan pánev
fuel palivo
full (filled) plný;
   (after meal) obsazený
fun zábava
furniture nábytek
fuse pojistka

G

game (sport) zápas; **(toy)** hra
garage (parking) garáž;
   (repair) servis
garbage bag pytel na odpadky
garden zahrada
gas benzín
gas station benzínová pumpa
gate (airport) východ
gauze gáza
genuine originál
gift dárek
girl děvče
girlfriend milenka
give dát

gland žláza
glass (drinking) sklenice
glasses (optical) brýle
glove rukavice
go (on foot) jít; **(by vehicle)** jet
goggles potápěčské brýle
gold zlato
golf golf
golf course golfové hřiště
good dobrý; **(delicious)** výborný
grandparents prarodiče
grass tráva
gray šedý
great úžasný
green zelený
greengrocer [BE] ovoce
   a zelenina
grocery store potraviny
ground (earth) zem
ground floor [BE] přízemí
groundcloth [BE] podlážka
groundsheet podlážka
group skupina
guarantee záruka
guest house penzión
guide průvodce
guided tour prohlídka s průvodcem
guided walk vycházka s průvodcem
guitar kytara
gynecologist gynekolog

H

hair vlasy
hairdresser kadeřník
hairdryer fén
hairspray lak na vlasy
half půl
hammer kladivo
hand (body) ruka

handbag kabelka
handicapped *adj* tělesně postižený
handicrafts řemesla
handkerchief kapesník
hand-washable prát v ruce
hanger ramínko
hangover *n* kocovina
happen stát se
harbor přístav
hard (firm) tvrdý;
   (difficult) obtížný
hat klobouk
have mít
hay fever senná rýma
head hlava
health zdraví
health food store zdravá výživa
health insurance zdravotní
   pojištění
hear slyšet
hearing aid sluchadlo
heart *n* srdce; **(cards)** srdce
heart attack infarkt
heat topení
heavy těžký
height výška
hemorrhoids hemoroidy
here (motion) sem;
   (place) tady
hernia kýla
high vysoký
highway dálnice
hiking *n* pěší turistika
hiking gear vybavení na turistiku
hill kopec
hire půjčit
historic site památková oblast
hobby (pastime) koníček
hold (wait) počkat

hole díra
holiday [BE] dovolená
holiday resort [BE] rekreační středisko
home domů
honeymoon svatebná cestě
hopefully snad
horse kůň
horse racing dostihy
hospital nemocnice
hot (temperature) horký; **(weather)** horko
hotel hotel
hour hodin
house dům
how jak
hundred sto
hunger hlad
hungry hladový
hurt bolet
husband manžel

I

ice led
icy zledovatělý
identification identifikace
ill nemocný
illegal nezákonné
imitation napodobenina
in (place) v; **(within a period of time)** za
include zahrnovat
incredible neuvěřitelný
indicate ukázat
indigestion porucha trávení
indoor pool krytý bazén
inexpensive levný
infection infekce
inflammation zánět

informal (dress) neformální
information informace
information office turistická kancelář
injection injekce
innocent nevinný
insect hmyz
insect bite štípanec
insect repellent repelent proti hmyzu
inside uvnitř
insomnia nespavost
instead místo
instructions návod
instructor instruktor
insulin inzulín
insurance (car) pojištění; **(company)** pojišťovna
insurance card pojistka
insurance certificate [BE] pojistka
insurance claim pojistná škoda
interest (hobby) zájem
interesting zajímavý
International Student Card mezinárodní studentský průkaz
internet internet
internet cafe internetová kavárna
interpreter tlumočník
intersection křižovatka
into do
invite pozvat
iodine jód
Ireland Irsko
item předmět
itemized bill rozepsaný účet
itch svědět

J

jacket sako
jaw čelist
jazz džez
jeans džíny
jet lag časový posun
jeweler klenoty mpl
job práce
join přidat
joint kloub
joke vtip
journalist novinář
journey cesta
jug (water) džbánek
junction křižovatka

K

keep nechat si
kerosene petrolej
kettle konvice
key klíč m
key card klíčová karta
key ring přívěsek ke klíčům
kiddie pool dětský bazén
kidney ledvina
kilometer kilometr
kind (pleasant) hodný
kiss *n* políbení; *v* políbit
kitchen kuchyně
kitchen foil [BE] alobal
knee koleno
knife nůž
know znát
kosher košer

L

label nálepka
lace krajka
ladder žebřík

lake jezero
lamp lampa
land (airplane) přistát
language course jazykový kurz
large velký
last *adj* poslední; *v* vydržet
late pozdě
laundromat prádelna
laundry facilities prádelna
lavatory záchod
lawyer právník
laxative projímadlo
lead *v* vést
leak *n* prosakování;
    v **(roof, pipe)** téct
learn učit se
leather kůže
leave (aircraft) odlétat; **(by vehicle)**
    odjíždět; **(on foot)** odejít
left vlevo
left-luggage office [BE] úschovna
    zavazadel
leg noha
legal legální
lend půjčit
length délka
lens (camera) čočka
lens cap víčko na čočku
less méně
lesson hodina
letter dopis
level *adj* rovný
library knihovna
life život
life boat záchranný člun
life jacket záchranná vesta
lifeguard plavčík jacket
lift [BE] výtah;
    (hitchhiking) svezení

lift pass permanentka na vlek
light (color) světlý; **(weight)** lehký;
  (electric) světlo
lightbulb žárovka
lighter (cigarette) zapalovač
like líbit; **(want)** chtít;
  (activities) mít rád
line (subway) trasa
linen len
lip ret
lipstick rtěnka
liquor store obchod lihovinami
liter litr
little (small) malý
live žít
liver játra
living room obývací pokoj
lobby (theater, hotel) vestibul
local místní
lock *n* zámek; *v* zamknout
log on zalogovat
long dlouhý
long-distance bus dálkový autobus
long-sighted [BE] dalekozraký
look hledat
loose volný
lorry [BE] nákladní auto
lose ztratit
lost property office [BE] ztráty
  a nálezy
lost-and-found ztráty a nálezy
lot hodně
loud hlasitý
love milovat
lovely krásně
low nízký
luck štěstí
luggage zavazadla
luggage cart vozík na zavazadla

luggage trolley [BE] vozík
  na zavazadla
lump boule
lung plíce
lunch oběd

M

madam paní
magazine časopis
magnificent velkolepý
machine washable prát v pračce
maid (hotel) pokojská;
  (home) služebná
mail *n* pošta; *v* poslat
mailbox poštovní schránka
main hlavní
make-up make•up
male *adj* mužský; *n* muž
mallet palice
man pán
manager vedoucí
manicure manikúra
manual (car) manuální
many mnoho
map mapa
market tržnice
married (man) ženatý;
  (woman) vdaná
mascara řasenka
mask (diving) potápěčská
  maska
mass mše
massage masáž
match (game) zápas
matches zápalky
mattress matrace
maybe možná
mean *v* mínit
measure změřit

measurement míra
medication lék
medicine lék
medium (size) střední
meet setkat se
mechanic mechanik
member člen
menu jídelní lístek
message vzkaz
metal kov
microwave (oven) mikrovlnná trouba
midday [BE] poledne
midnight půlnoc
migraine migréna
million milión
mini-bar minibar
minute minuta
mirror zrcadlo
missing chybět
mistake (error) chyba; **(misunderstanding)** omyl
mobile phone [BE] mobilní telefon
moisturizer (cream) zvlhčující krém
monastery klášter
money peníze
money order poštovní poukázka
month měsíc
moped moped
more více
mosque mešita
mosquito bite štípnutí komárem
mother matka
motion sickness cestovní nemoc
motor boat motorový člun
motorcycle motocykl
motorway [BE] dálnice
mountain hora

mountain bike horské kolo
mountain pass horský průsmyk
mountain range horské pásmo
mouth ústa
movie film
movie theater kino
mugging přepadení
much hodně
muscle sval
museum muzeum
music hudba
musician hudebník

N

name jméno
napkin ubrousek
nappy [BE] plenka
narrow úzký
national národní
nationality státní příslušnost
nature přirozenost
nature reserve přírodní rezervace
nausea žaludeční nevolnost
near blízko
near-sighted krátkozraký
necessary nutný
neck (head) krk
necklace náhrdelník
need *n* nutnost; *v* potřebovat
nerve nerv
nervous system nervový systém
never nikdy
new nový
New Zealand Nový Zéland
newspaper noviny
newsstand novinový stánek
next (in a row) další; **(in a row)** nejbližší; **(in time)** příští

nice hezký
night noc
night club noční klub
noisy hlučný
non-alcoholic nealkoholický
none žádný
non-smoking nekuřáci
noon poledne
normal běžný
north sever
nose nos
nothing nic
notify uvědomit
now nyní
number číslo
nurse zdravotní sestra
nylon nylon

O

occasionally občas
occupied obsazený
office kancelář
off-licence [BE] obchod lihovinami
off-peak mimo špičku
often často
oil olej
old starý
old town staré město
on v
once jednou
one-way ticket (train) jízdenka jedním směrem; **(plane)** letenka jedním směrem
open *adj* otevřený; *v* otvírat
opening hours otevírací doba
opera opera
opera house operní divadlo
operation (medical) operace
opposite naproti

optician optik
or nebo
orange (color) oranžový
order objednat
organized organizovaný
orchestra orchestr
outdoor venkovní
outdoor pool venkovní bazén
outrageous nestydatý
outside venku
oval oválný
oven trouba
overheat přehřátí
overnight přes noc
owe dlužit
own *v* vlastnit

P

pacifier dudlík
pack balit
package balík
paddling pool [BE] dětský bazén
padlock visací zámek
pail kyblík
pain bolest
painkiller lék proti bolesti
paint malovat
painting malířství obraz
palace palác
palpitations bušení srdce
panorama panoráma
pants kalhoty
panty hose punčochové kalhoty
paralysis ochrnutí
parcel [BE] balík
parents rodiče
park park
parking lot parkoviště
parking meter parkovací hodiny

parliament building budova parlamentu
partner (male) partner; **(female)** partnerka
party (social) společnost; **(event)** večírek
passport pas
pastry shop cukrárna
patch *v* spravit
patient *n* pacient
pavement chodník
pay zaplatit
pay phone telefonní budka
payment platba
peak vrchol
pearl perla
pedestrian pěšák
pedestrian crossing přechod pro chodce
pedestrian precinct [BE] pěší zóna
pedestrian zone pěší zóna
pen pero
people lidé
perhaps možná
period (menstrual) menstruace
petrol [BE] benzín
petrol station [BE] benzínová pumpa
pewter cín
pharmacy lékárna
phone *v* telefonovat
phone card telefonní karta
photo vyfotografovat
photo fotografie
photocopier kopírka
phrase věta
phrase book konverzační příručka
pick up (something) vyzvednout si
picnic piknik

picnic area místo na piknik
piece kousek
pill tableta; **(contraceptive)** antikoncepční pilulka
pillow polštář
pillow case povlak na polštář
pilot light plamínek
pink růžový
pipe (smoking) dýmka
plan plán
plane letadlo
plant *n* rostlina
plaster [BE] náplast
plastic bag igelitová taška
plate talíř
platform nástupiště
platinum platina
play *n* představení; *v* hrát
playground dětské hřiště
pleasant příjemný
please prosím
plug zástrčka
pneumonia zápal plíc
point *v* ukázat
poison jed
police policie report
police report zpráva od policie
police station policejní stanice
pollen count hladina pylu
polyester polyester
pond rybník
popular populární
port (harbor) přístav
porter nosič
portion porce
post [BE] *n* pošta; *v* podat na poště
postbox [BE] poštovní schránka
postcard pohlednice
pottery keramika

pound (sterling) libra
power energie
pregnant těhotná
prescribe předepsat
prescription předpis
present (gift) dárek
press vyžehlit
pretty hezký
price cena
prison vězení
profession povolání
program program
pronounce vyslovit
pub hospoda
public *n* veřejnost
pump (gas station) pumpa
puncture píchlý
pure čistý
purse kabelka
pushchair [BE] kočárek

Q

quality *adj* kvalitní
quarter čtvrt
queue [BE] *n* fronta; *v* stát ve frontě
quick rychlý
quiet tichý

R

racetrack závodní dráha
racket (tennis, squash) raketa
railway [BE] železnice
railway station [BE] nádraží
rain *n* déšť; *v* pršet
raincoat pláštěnka
rape znásilnění
rapids peřej
rash vyrážka
razor holicí strojek

ready hotový
real (genuine) pravý
rear zadní
receipt (payment) stvrzenka
reception (desk) recepce
receptionist recepční
recommend doporučit
reduction (in price) sleva
refrigerator lednice
refund *n* náhrada; *v* vrátit peníze
region (geographical) oblast
registered mail doporučeně
registration form registrační karta
regular obyčejný
reliable spolehlivý
religion vyznání
rent půjčit
rental car auto z půjčovny
repair *v* opravit
repeat zopakovat
replacement *adj* náhradní
replacement part náhradní díl
report (crime) ohlásit
require potřebovat
required (necessary) nutný
reservation rezervace;
   (on a train) místenka
reserve zamluvit
rest *v* odpočívat
restaurant restaurace
retired v důchodu
return vrátit se; **(give back)** vrátit
return ticket [BE] (train) zpáteční
   jízdenka; **(plane)** zpáteční letenka
rheumatism revmatismus
rib žebro
right správný
right of way (in a car) přednost;
   (access) přístupný

ring prsten
river řeka
road silnice
road map automapa
robbery loupež
romantic romantický
roof (house, car) střecha
room pokoj
rope lano
round kulatý
round-trip ticket zpáteční lístek
route cesta
rude nezdvořilý
ruins zříceniny
rush hour špička

S

safe *adj* **(not dangerous)** bezpečný;
  (feeling) bezpečně; *n* sejf
safety bezpečí
sales tax DPH
same stejný
sand písek
sandals sandály
sanitary napkin dámská vložka
sanitary pad [BE] dámská vložka
satin satén
satisfied spokojený
sauna sauna
scarf šátek
scissors nůžky
Scotland Skotsko
screwdriver šroubovák
sea moře
seasickness mořskou nemoc
season ticket sezónní lístek
seat (on train, etc.) místo;
  (theater) sedadlo
second class druhá třída

secretary sekretářka
sedative sedativum
see vidět; **(inspect)** podívat se
self-employed soukromník
self-service (gas station) samoobsluha
sell prodávat
send poslat
senior citizen starší občan
separately samostatně
serious závažný
service (in restaurant) obsluha;
  (religious) bohoslužba
shade odstín
shallow mělký
shampoo šampon
share rozdělovat se
sharp ostrý
shaving cream krém na holení
sheet (bed) povlečení
shirt (men's) košile
shock (electric) šok
shoe bot
shoe store obchod s obuví
shopping area oblast s obchody
shopping basket nákupní košík
shopping centre [BE] obchodní centrum
shopping mall obchodní centrum
short (opp. long) krátký;
  (opp. tall) nízký; **(height)** malý
shorts krátké kalhoty
short-sighted [BE] krátkozraký
shoulder rameno
shovel lopatka
show ukázat
shower sprcha
shut *adj* zavřený; *v* zavírat
sights pamětihodnosti
sightseeing tour prohlídka
sign (road sign) značka

signpost [BE] ukazatel
silk hedvábí
silver stříbro
singer zpěvák
single (unmarried) svobodný
single room jednolůžkový pokoj
single ticket [BE] **(train)** jízdenka
  jedním směrem; **(plane)** letenka
  jedním
  směrem
sink umyvadlo
sister sestra
sit sedět
size velikost
skates brusle
ski n lyže; v lyžovat
ski boots lyžařské boty
ski poles lyžařské hole
skin pokožka
skirt sukně
sleep spát
sleeping bag spací pytel
sleeping car lůžkový vůz
sleeping pill prášek na spaní
sleeve rukáv
slice plátek
slippers papuče
slow pomalý
small malý
small change drobné
smell zápach
smoke v zapálit
smoking kuřáci
sneakers tenisky
snorkel šnorchl
snow n sníh; v sněžit
soap mýdlo
soccer fotbal
socket zástrčka

socks ponožky
something něco
sometimes někdy
son syn
soon brzo
sore bolí
sour kyselý
south jih
souvenir suvenýr
space místo
spare (part) náhradní; **(extra)** navíc
speak mluvit
special zvláštní
specialist specialista
specimen vzorek
spell hláskovat
spend (time, money) strávit;
  (waste) utratit
spicy kořeněný
sponge houba
spoon lžíce
sport sport
sporting goods store sportovní
  potřeby
sports club sportovní klub
spot (place, site) místo
sprained vyvrtnutý
square náměstí
stadium stadion
staff personál
stain skvrna
stairs schodiště
stamp známka
stand stát
standby ticket lístek na čekací
  listině
start začínat
statement (police) prohlášení
stationery store papírnictví

statue socha
stay (remain) zůstat
steal ukrást
sterilizing solution sterilizační roztok
stockings punčochy
stolen *adj* ukradený
stomach žaludek
stomachache bolení břicha
stop (bus) stanice; *v* stavět
store guide informační tabule
stormy bouřka
stove vařič
strange divný
straw brčko
stream potok
stroller kočárek
strong silný
student student
study studovat
style styl
subtitled s titulky
subway metro
subway map plán metra
subway station stanice metra
suggest doporučit
suit (man's) oblek; **(woman's)** kostým
suitable vhodný
summer léto
sun slunce
sunbathe opalovat se
sunglasses sluneční brýle
sunstroke úžeh
superb skvělý
supermarket samoobsluha
supervision dozor
supplement přirážka
suppository čípek
sure určitě

surname příjmení
sweater svetr
sweatshirt tričko
sweet (taste) sladký
swelling oteklina
swim suit
swimming pool bazén
swimming trunks pánské plavky
swimsuit dámské plavky
swollen oteklý
symptom (illness) příznak
synagogue synagoga
synthetic umělý

T
table stůl
take (medicine) užívat; **(carry)** vzít
talk mluvit
tall vysoký
tampon tampón
tan opálení
taxi taxík
taxi rank [BE] stanoviště taxíků
taxi stand stanoviště taxíků
teacher učitel
team tým
teddy bear medvídek
telephone *n* telefon; *v* zatelefonovat
telephone bill účet za telefon
telephone booth telefonní budka
telephone call telefonický hovor
telephone number telefonní číslo
temperature (body) teplota
temple chrám
temporarily dočasně
tennis tenis
tennis court tenisový kurt

tent stan
tent pegs stanové kolíčky
terrace terasa
terrible hrozný
terrific báječně
theater divadlo
theft krádež
then (time) potom
there tam
thermometer teploměr
thermos termoska
thick silný
thief zloděj
thigh stehno
thin (not thick) slabý;
  (narrow) tenký; **(weight)** hubený
thirsty žíznivý
throat krk
through přes
thumb palec
ticket (train) jízdenka;
  (plane) letenka; **(theater, etc.)**
  lístek
ticket office pokladna
tie kravata
tight těsný
tights punčochové kalhoty
tin opener [BE] otvírač na plechovky
tired unavený
tissue papírový kapesník
to (place, purpose) k
tobacco tabák
tobacconist tabák
today dnes
toe prst na noze
toilet záchod
toilet paper toaletní papír
tomorrow zítra
tongue jazyk

tonight dnes večer
too (extreme) moc
tooth zub
toothbrush kartáček na zuby
toothpaste zubní pasta
torch ruční svítilna
torn natržený
tough (food) tuhý
tour zájezd
tour guide průvodce
tourist turista
tourist office turistická kancelář
tow truck havarijní služba
towel ručník
tower věž
town město
town hall radnice
toy hračka
traditional tradiční
traffic doprava
traffic jam dopravní zácpa
traffic offence [BE] dopravní
  přestupek
traffic violation dopravní
  přestupek
trailer obytný přívěs
train vlak
train station nádraží
tram tramvaj
transit v projíždět
translate přeložit
translation překlad
translator překladatel
travel agency cestovní kancelář
travel sickness cestovní nemoc
travelers check cestovní šek
travellers cheque [BE] cestovní
  šek
tray podnos

tree strom
trim zastřihnout
trip cesta
trolley vozík
trousers [BE] kalhoty
truck nákladní automobil
T-shirt triko
tumor nádor
tunnel tunel
turn down (volume) stáhnout
turn off vypnout
turn on zapnout
turn up (volume) zesílit
TV televize
tweezers pinzeta
type *n* typ
typical typický

U

ugly ošklivý
ulcer vřed
umbrella (sun) slunečník;
 (rain) deštník
uncle strýc
under pod
underground [BE] metro
underground station [BE] stanice
 metra
understand rozumět
underwear spodní prádlo
undress svléknout se
uneven (ground) hrbolatý
unfortunately bohužel
uniform uniforma
unit (for a phone card) jednotka
United Kingdom Velké Británie
United States Spojené Státy
unleaded (gas) bezolovnatý
unlimited mileage počet kilometrů

není omezen
unlock odemknout
unpleasant nepříjemný
unscrew odšroubovat
until do
upper (berth) nahoře
upset stomach bolení břicha
urine moč
use *n* potřeba; *v* použít
utensils příbory

V

vacant volný
vacation dovolená
vaginal infection vaginální
 infekce
valet service parkovací služby
valid platný
validate (tickets) potvrdit
valley údolí
valuable cenný
valve uzavírací kohout
VAT [BE] DPH
VAT receipt [BE] daň z přidané
 hodnoty
vegetarian vegetariánský
vein žíla
venereal disease pohlavní
 nemoc
ventilator větrák
very velmi
video game video hra
viewpoint vyhlídka
village vesnice
vineyard vinice
visa vízum
visit *v* navštívit; **(see sights)**
 podívat se
visiting hours návštěvní hodiny

volleyball volejbal
voltage napětí
vomit zvracet

W

wait počkat
waiter vrchní
waiting room čekárna
wake vzbudit
wake-up call buzení telefonem
walking route turistická cesta
wallet peněženka
war memorial památník obětem války
ward (hospital) oddělení
warm teplý
washing machine pračka
wasp vosa
water voda
waterfall vodopád
waterproof vodotěsný
waterproof jacket nepromokavá bunda
watch *n* hodinky
wave vlna
wear mít na sobě
weather počasí
weather forecast předpověď počasí
wedding svatba
week týden
weekend víkend
weekend rate víkendová sazba
west západ
wet mokrý
wetsuit neoprenový oblek
wheelchair kolečková židle
when kdy
where kde

which který
who kdo
whose čí
wide široký
wife manželka
wildlife divoká příroda
wind vítr
window okno; (store) výloha
window seat sedadlo u okna
wireless internet bezdrátový internet
with s
withdraw vyzvednout
within (time) do
without bez
witness svědek
wood les
wool vlna
work (function) fungovat
worse horší
write napsat
wrong chybný

X

x-ray rentgen

Y

yacht jachta
year rok
yes ano
yesterday včera
young mladý
youth hostel mládežnická ubytovna

Z

zero nula
zipper zip
zoo zoo

Czech–English Dictionary

A

a and
adaptér adapter
adresa address
aerolinka airline
akumulátor battery (car)
ale but
alergický allergic
alergie allergy
alkoholický alcoholic (drink)
alobal aluminum [kitchen BE] foil
americký *adj* American
Američan *n* American
anestetický anesthetic
anestetikum anasthetia
anglický *adj* English
angličtina English (language)
Anglie England
Anglik *n* English
ano yes
antibiotik antibiotic
antikoncepce contraceptive
antikoncepční pilulka pill
  (contraceptive)
architekt architect
artritid arthritis
asi about (approximately)
aspirin aspirin
astma asthma
atletika athletics
audio průvodce audio guide
Austrálie Australia
auto car
auto z půjčovny rental car
autobus bus
autobusová zastávka bus stop

autobusové nádraží bus station
automapa road map
autorizovat accept
až k up to

B

báječně terrific
balet ballet
balík package
balit pack
balkón balcony
banka bank
bankomat ATM
bar bar
barva color
baterie battery
bavlna cotton
bazén swimming pool
během during
benzín gas [petrol BE]
benzínová pumpa gas [petrol BE]
  station
bez without
bezolovnatý unleaded
bezpečí safety
bezpečně *adv* safe (feeling)
bezpečný *adj* safe (not dangerous)
běžný normal
bikiny bikini
bitevní pole battle site
blecha flea
blízko *adv* close (near)
blůza blouse
bohoslužba service (religious)
bohužel unfortunately
bolení břicha stomachache

bolest pain
bolest zad backache
bolet hurt
bolí sore
bot shoe
botanická zahrada botanical garden
boty boots
boule lump
bouřka stormy
bratr brother
brčko straw
britský British
broušené sklo cut glass
brož brooch
brožura brochure
brusle skates
brýle glasses (optical)
bryndáček bib
brzdy brakes (car, bicycle)
brzo soon
budík alarm clock
budova building
budova parlamentu parliament building
budovat built
bušení srdce palpitations
buzení telefonem wake-up call
byt apartment
být be

C

cédéčko CD
celní prohlídka customs
cena *n* cost; price
cenný valuable
centrum center of town
centrum města downtown

cesta course (track, path); route; trip
cestovní kancelář travel agency
cestovní nemoc motion sickness
cestovní šek travelers check [cheque BE]
cigareta cigarette
cín pewter
cítit feel
cukrárna pastry shop
cyklistická stezka cycle route
cyklistika cycling
Czech *n* Czech

Č

časopis magazine
časový posun jet lag
částka amount (money)
často *adv* often
čekárna waiting room
čelist jaw
čepice cap (clothing)
čerstvý fresh
Česká Republika Czech Republic
český *adj* Czech
čí whose
čípek suppository
číslo number
číslo kreditní karty credit card number
čistírna dry cleaner
čistý *adj* clean, pure
člen member
čočka lens (camera)
čtrnáct dní fortnight
čtvrt quarter

D

dabovaný dubbed
dalekohled binoculars
dalekozraký far-sighted [long-sighted BE]
dálkový autobus long-distance bus
dálnice highway [motorway BE]
další next (subsequent)
dámská vložka sanitary napkin [pad BE]
dámské plavky swimsuit
dárek gift
dát give
dávka course (medication)
dcera daughter
délka length
den day
denně daily
denní jízdenka day ticket
deodorant deodorant
destilovaná voda distilled water
déšť n rain
deštník umbrella (rain)
dětská láhev baby bottle
dětská postýlka crib [child's cot BE]
dětská sedačka child's seat
dětské hřiště playground
dětský bazén kiddie [paddling BE] pool
děvče girl
diabetik diabetic
diamant diamond
dieselový motor diesel (vehicle)
dieta diet
digitální fotoaparát digital camera
díra hole
dirigent conductor
diskotéka dance club

dítě child; baby
divadlo theater
dívat se browse
divný strange
divoká příroda wildlife
dlouhý long
dlužit owe
dnes today
dnes večer tonight
do by (time); for (towards); into; until
dobrý good
dobře fine (well)
dočasně temporarily
doktor doctor
dolar dollar (U.S.)
domů home
dopis letter
doporučeně registered mail
doporučit recommend
doprava traffic
dopravní přestupek traffic violation [offence BE]
dopravní zácpa traffic jam
doprovodit accompany
doručit deliver
dospělý n adult
dost enough
dostihová dráha race track
dostihy horse racing
doutník cigar
dovolená vacation [holiday BE]
dozor supervision
DPH sales tax [VAT BE]
drahý expensive
drobné n change (coins)
drogerie drugstore
druhá třída second class
dřevěné uhlí charcoal

dudlík pacifier [dummy BE]
dům house
dvě lůžka twin beds
dveře door
dýchat breathe
dýmka pipe (smoking)
džbánek carafe; jug (water)
džez jazz
džínsovina denim
džíny jeans

E

ekonomická třída economy class
elastický *adj* elastic
elektrické zásuvka electrical outlet
elektrický holicí strojek electric razor
elektronická pošta e-mail
elektronický electronic
elektronický lístek e-ticket
email enamel
emailová adresa e-mail address
energie power
epileptik *n* epileptic
eskalátor escalator

F

faktor factor (sunscreen)
fax fax
fén hairdryer
film movie [film BE];
  film (camera)
filtr filter
firma company (business)
formální oblečení formal dress
formulář form
fotbal soccer [football BE]
fotoaparát camera
fotografie photo

foyer foyer (hotel, theater)
fronta *n* line [queue BE]
fungovat work (function)

G

galerie art gallery
garáž garage (parking)
gáza gauze
golf golf
golfové hříště golf course
golfové hůl club (golf)
gynekolog gynecologist

H

hadr na nádobí dishcloth
hasicí přístroj fire extinguisher
hasiči fire department
  [brigade BE]
havarijní služba tow truck
hedvábí silk
hemoroidy hemorrhoids
hezký nice; pretty
hlad hunger
hladina pylu pollen count
hladový hungry
hlasitý loud
hláskovat spell
hlava head
hlavní main
hledat look
hluboký deep
hlučný noisy
hluchý deaf
hmyz insect
hodin hour
hodina lesson
hodinky *n* watch
hodiny clock

hodně much
hodný kind (pleasant)
holčička girl (little girl)
holicí strojek razor
holičství barber
hora mountain
horečka fever
horko *adv* hot (weather)
horký *adj* hot (temperature)
horské kolo mountain bike
horské pásmo mountain range
horský průsmyk mountain pass
horší worse
hořký bitter
hospoda pub
hotel hotel
hotovost cash (money)
hotový ready
houba sponge
hra game (toy)
hračka toy
hrad castle
hrát *v* play
hrbolatý uneven (ground)
hrozný terrible
hřbitov cemetery
hřeben comb
hubený thin (weight)
hudba music
hudebník musician

CH

chata cottage
chemicky vyčistit *v* dry clean
chlad *n* cold
chladný cold (weather)
chlapec boy
chodidlo foot
chodník pavement

chrám temple
chřipka flu (influenza)
chtít like (want)
chuť k jídlu appetite
chutný delicious
chyba error
chyba mistake (error)
chybět missing
chybný wrong

I

identifikace identification
igelitová taška plastic bag
infarkt heart attack
infekce infection
informace information
informační tabule store guide
injekce injection
instruktor instructor
internet internet
internetová kavárna internet cafe
invalida *n* disabled
inzulín insulin
Irsko Ireland

J

jachta yacht
jak how
jakýkoliv any
jaro spring
játra liver
jazyk tongue
jazykový kurz language course
jed poison
jedním směrem one-way (ticket)
jednodenní výlet day trip
jednolůžkový pokoj single room
jednotka unit (for a phone card)
jednou once

jeho his
její her(s)
jejich their(s)
jeskyně cave
jet drive
jezero lake
jídelna dining room
jídelní lístek menu
jídelní vůz dining car
jídlo food
jih south
jiný another
jíst eat
jít go (on foot)
jízdenka ticket (train)
jízdenka jedním směrem one-way [single BE] ticket (train)
jízdní kolo bicycle
jméno name
jód iodine

K

k to (place, purpose)
kabát coat
kadeřnictví hairdresser
kalendář calendar
kalhoty pants [trousers BE]
kamaše leggings
Kanada Canada
kanál canal
kancelář office
kapesník handkerchief
kapky do uší ear drops
karta card
kartáček na zuby toothbrush
kasino casino
kašel *n* cough
kašlat *v* cough
kašna fountain

katedrála cathedral
kavárna café
každý every
kde where
kdo who
kdy when
kempink campsite
keramika pottery
kilometr kilometer
kino movie theater [cinema BE]
kladivo hammer
klášter monastery
klenotník jeweler
klíč key
klíčová karta key card
klimatizace air conditioning
klobouk hat
kloub joint
kniha book
knihkupectví bookstore
knihovna library
knír moustache
knoflík button
koberec carpet
kocovina *n* hangover
kočárek stroller [pushchair BE]
kojenecká výživa baby food
kojit breastfeed
kolečková židle wheelchair
kolem around (time)
koleno knee
koncert concert
koncertní síň concert hall
končit end
kondicionér conditioner (hair)
kondom condom
koníček hobby (pastime)
kontaktní čočka contact lens
kontrolovat *v* check

konverzační příručka phrase book
konvice kettle
konzulát consulate
kopec hill
kopie copy
kopírka photocopier
koruna crown (royal; Czech currency)
korunka crown (dental)
kořeněný spicy
kosmetika cosmetics
kost bone
kostel church
kostky dice
kostým suit (woman's)
košer kosher
košík basket
košíková basketball
košile shirt (men's)
kotel boiler
koupat *v* bath
koupelna bathroom
koupit buy
kousek piece
kov metal
krabička box
krádež theft
krajka lace
krásně *adv* lovely
krásný *adj* beautiful
krátké kalhoty shorts
krátkozraký near-sighted
   [short-sighted BE]
krátký short (not long)
kravata tie
krb fire
kreditní karta credit card
krém na holení shaving cream
krev blood
krevní tlak blood pressure

krk neck; throat
kromě except
krvácet bleed
krytý bazén indoor pool
křeče cramps
křišťál crystal
křižovatka intersection; junction
který which
kuchař *n* cook (chef)
kuchyňské vybavení cooking
   facilities
kulatý round
kulturní přehled entertainment
   guide
kůň horse
kurz exchange rate
kuřáci smoking
kuvert cover charge
kůže leather
kvalitní *adj* quality
květ flower
květiny florist
kyblík bucket
kýla hernia
kyselý sour
kytara guitar

L

láhev bottle
lahůdky delicatessen
lak na vlasy hair spray
lampa lamp
lano rope
látka fabric
led ice
lednice refrigerator
ledvina kidney
legální legal
lehký light (weight)

lék medication
lék proti bolesti painkiller
lékárna pharmacy [chemist BE]
len linen
les forest
let číslo flight number
letadlo plane
letadlová nemoc air-sickness
letecká pošta airmail
letenka ticket (plane)
letenka jedním směrem one-way
    [single BE] ticket (plane)
letiště airport
léto summer
levný cheap
líbit like
libra pound (sterling)
lidé people
linka extension
lístek ticket (theater)
lístek na čekací listině standby ticket
litr liter
lopatka shovel
loupež robbery
ložnice bedroom
lunapark amusement park
lůžko berth
lůžkový vůz sleeping car
lyžařské boty ski boots
lyžařské hole ski poles
lyže n ski
lyžovat v ski
lžíce spoon

M

make-up make-up
malířství obraz painting
málo few
malovat paint

malý little (small); short (height);
mandle tonsils
manikúra manicure
manuální manual (car)
manžel husband
manželka wife
manželská postel double bed
mapa map
masáž massage
matka mother
matrace mattress
měď copper
medvídek teddy bear
mechanik mechanic
mělký shallow
měna currency
méně less
menstruace period (menstrual)
měsíc month
město town
mešita mosque
mezi between (time)
mezinárodní studentský průkaz
    International Student Card
míč ball
migréna migraine
mikrovlnná trouba microwave (oven)
milenec boyfriend
milenka girlfriend
milión million
milovat love
mimo špičku off-peak
mince coin
minibar mini-bar
mínit v mean
minuta minute
míra measurement
miska bowl
místenka reservation (on a train)

místo instead; seat (on train); spot (place, site)
místo na piknik picnic area
místo u uličky aisle seat
mít have
mít na sobě wear
mít rád enjoy
mládežnická ubytovna youth hostel
mladý young
mlhavo foggy
mluvit talk; speak
mnoho many
mobilní telefon cell [mobile BE] phone
moč urine
močový měchýř bladder
modrý blue
modřina bruise
mokrý wet
moped moped
moře sea
mořskou nemoc seasickness
most bridge
motocykl motorcycle
motor engine
motorový člun motor boat
moucha fly (insect)
možná maybe
mráz frost
mraznička freezer
mše mass
muzeum museum
muž *n* male
muži men (toilets)
mužský *adj* male
mýdlo soap

N

na for (time)
na zdraví cheers

nábytek furniture
nadobá dish (tableware)
nádor tumor
nádraží train [railway BE] station
nadváha excess luggage
nafta diesel (fuel)
nafukovací matrace air mattress
náhrada *n* refund
náhradní spare (part)
náhradní díl replacement part
náhrdelník necklace
najít find
nakažlivý contagious
nákladní auto truck [lorry BE]
nakojit feed
nákupní košík shopping basket
naléhavý *adj* emergency
nálepka label
náležet belong
náměstí square
napětí voltage
náplast bandage [plaster BE]
napodobenina imitation
naproti opposite
napsat write
náramek bracelet
narodit se born
národní national
narozeniny birthday
nashledanou bye
nástěnka bulletin board
nástupiště platform
náš our(s)
naštěstí fortunately
natržený torn
náušnice earring
navíc spare (extra)
navlhčené ubrousek baby wipe
návod instructions

návštěvní hodiny visiting hours
navštívit *v* visit
nealkoholický non-alcoholic
nebezpečný dangerous
nebo or
něco something
neformální informal (dress)
nehoda accident (road)
nechat si keep
nejbližší next (in a row)
někdy sometimes
nekuřáci non-smoking
nemocnice hospital
nemocný sick [ill BE]
nemrznoucí směs antifreeze
neoprenový oblek wetsuit
nepřetržitý constant
nepříjemný unpleasant
nerv nerve
nervový systém nervous system
nespavost insomnia
nestydatý outrageous
neúmyslně accidentally
neuvěřitelný incredible
nevinný innocent
nezákonné illegal
nezbytný essential
nezdvořilý rude
nic nothing
někdo anyone
nikdy never
nízký low; short (opp. tall)
noc night
noční klub night club
noha leg
nos nose
nosič porter
nouzový východ emergency exit
novinář journalist

novinový stánek newsstand
noviny newspaper
nový new
Nový Zéland New Zealand
nudný boring
nutnost *n* need
nutný necessary
nůž knife
nůžky scissors
nylon nylon
nyní now

O

obálka envelope
občas occasionally
obdivuhodný amazing
oběd lunch
obchod lihovinami liquor store [off-licence BE]
obchod s obuví shoe store
obchodní centrum shopping mall [centre BE]
obchodní dům department store
obchodní třída business class
objednat order
oblačný cloudy
oblast region (geographical)
oblast s obchody shopping area
oblek suit (man's)
oblíbený favorite
obličej face
obroučky frame (glasses)
obsahovat contain
obsazený full (after meal); occupied
obsluha service (in restaurant)
obtížný hard (difficult)
obyčejný medium (position); regular
obytný přívěs trailer

obývací pokoj living room
od from (time)
odbarvovací prostředek bleach
oddělení ward (hospital)
odečíst deduct (money)
odejít leave (on foot)
odemknout unlock
oděvy clothing store
odjezdová hala departure lounge
odjíždět depart (train, bus)
odlétat depart (plane)
odpadky garbage [rubbish BE]
odpočívat v rest
odstín shade
odšroubovat unscrew
ohlásit report (crime)
ochrnutí paralysis
okenice shutter
okno window
olej oil
olej po opalování after-sun lotion
omlouvat apologize
omyl mistake (misunderstanding)
opálení tan
opalovat se sunbathe
opatrný careful
opera opera
operace operation (medical)
operní divadlo opera house
opravit repair
opravy repairs
optik optician
organizovaný organized
orchestr orchestra
originál genuine
ostrý sharp
ostřihat cut (hair)

osvědčení certificate
ošetřit obličej facial
ošklivý ugly
otec father
oteklina swelling
oteklý swollen
otevírací doba opening hours
otevřený adj open
otrava potravinami food poisoning
otřes mozku concussion
otvírač na láhve bottle opener
otvírač na plechovky can [tin BE] opener
otvírat v open
oválný oval
ovoce a zelenina fruit and vegetable store [greengrocer BE]

P

pacient n patient
palác palace
palec thumb
palice mallet
palivo fuel
palivové dříví wood
palubní n board
palubní vstupenka boarding card
památková oblast historic site
památník obětem války war memorial
pamětihodnosti sights
pán man
panenka doll
pánev frying pan
paní madam
paní na hlídání děti babysitter
panoráma panorama
pánské plavky swimming trunks
papírnictví stationery store

papírové ubrousky paper napkins
papírový kapesník tissue
papuče slippers
park park
parkovací hodiny parking meter
parkovací služby valet service
parkoviště parking lot
  [car park BE]
partner partner
pas passport
pásek belt
paže arm
pekařství bakery
pěna na vlasy hair mousse
peníze money
penzión guest house
perla pearl
permanentka na vlek lift pass
pero pen
personál staff
peřej rapids
peřina duvet
pěšák pedestrian
pěší turistika *n* hiking
pěší zóna pedestrian zone [precinct BE]
pěšina footpath
petrolej kerosene
píchlý flat [puncture BE]
piknik picnic
pinzeta tweezers
písek sand
pít *v* drink
pití *n* drink
plán plan
plán metra subway
  [underground BE] map
pláštěnka raincoat
platba payment
plátek slice

platina platinum
platný valid
plavčík jacket lifeguard
pláž beach
plenka diaper [nappy BE]
plíce lung
plný full (filled)
plomba filling (dental)
plyn butane gas
po after (time); around (place)
pobřeží coast
počasí weather
počet kilometrů není omezen
  unlimited mileage
počítač computer
počkat wait
pod under
podat na poště *v* post (send)
podívat se see (inspect); visit (see sights)
podlážka groundsheet
  [groundcloth BE]
podnos tray
podprsenka bra
podrobnosti details
pohlavní nemoc venereal disease
pohlednice postcard
pohodlný comfortable
pojistka insurance card
  [certificate BE]
pojistná škoda insurance claim
pojištění insurance (car)
pojišťovna insurance (company)
pokoj room
pokojská maid (hotel)
pokožka skin
pokuta fine (penalty)
pole field
poledne noon [midday BE]
políbení *n* kiss

políbit *v* kiss
policejní stanice police station
policie report police
polštář pillow
polyester polyester
pomalý slow
ponožky socks
popálenina *n* burn
popelnica garbage [dustbin BE]
popelník ashtray
popsat describe
populární popular
porce portion
porucha breakdown
porucha trávení indigestion
poschodí floor (level)
poslat *v* mail
poslední *adj* last
postel bed
poškodit damage
pošta *n* mail [post BE]
poštovní poukázka money order
poštovní schránka mailbox [postbox BE]
potápěčská maska mask (diving)
potápěčské brýle swimming goggles
potok stream
potom then (time)
potravinová fólie cling film
potraviny grocery store
potřeba *n* need; requirement
potvrdit confirm (reservation); validate (tickets)
použít *v* use
povětří *n* air
povlak na polštář pillow case
povlečení sheet (bed)
povolání profession
povolené zboží allowance
pozadu slow (clock)

pozdě late
pozvat invite
požár fire (disaster)
požární hlásič fire alarm
práce job
pračka washing machine
prádelna laundromat
prapodivný bizarre
prarodiče grandparents
prášek na praní washing powder
prášek na spaní sleeping pill
prát v pračce machine washable
prát v ruce hand-washable
právník lawyer
pravost authenticity
pravý authentic
prázdný empty
prodávat sell
program program
prohlášení statement (police)
prohlídka sightseeing tour
prohlídka s průvodcem guided tour
projímadlo laxative
projíždět *v* transit
proplatit *v* cash
prosakování *n* leak
prosím please
prosit ask (request)
prostor na přebalování changing facilities
prostředek na mytí nádobí dishwashing liquid
protéza denture
protože because
provize commission
prsa chest (body)
prso breast
prst finger
prst na noze toe

prsten ring
pršet v rain
průjem diarrhea
průvodce guide
první třída first class
přátelský friendly
přebalit dítě change (a baby)
před ago
před before (time)
předepsat prescribe
předmět item
přední adj front
přednost right of way (in a car)
předpis prescription
předpověď počasí weather forecast
představení n play
přehřátí overheat
přechod pro chodce pedestrian crossing
překlad translation
překladatel translator
přeložit translate
přepadení mugging
přes across
přes noc overnight
přestoupit change (transportation)
přibližně approximately
příbory cutlery
přidat join
přihlásit declare
příchuť flavor
příjemný pleasant
přijet arrive (car, train)
přijít call (shout)
příjmení surname
příklad example
přikrývka blanket
přikrývky a povlečení bedding
přiletět arrive (plane)

přímý direct (train, flight)
přirážka supplement
přírodní rezervace nature reserve
přirozenost nature
přistát land (airplane)
přístav harbor
přístupný right of way (access)
příští next (in time)
přitažlivý attractive
přítel friend
příušnice mumps
přívěsek ke klíčům key ring
přivést bring
přízemí first [ground BE] floor
příznak symptom (illness)
pták bird
ptát ask (question)
puchýř blister
půjčit borrow; hire; lend; rent
půjčovna aut car rental
půl half
půlnoc midnight
pumpa pump (gas station)
punčochové kalhoty pantyhose [tights BE]
punčochy stockings
pytel na odpadky garbage [rubbish BE] bag

R

radnice town hall
raketa racket (tennis, squash)
rakovina cancer (disease)
rameno shoulder
ramínko coat hanger
recepce reception (desk)
recepční receptionist
registrační karta registration form
rekreační středisko holiday resort

rentgen x-ray
repelent proti hmyzu insect repellent
restaurace restaurant
ret lip
revmatismus rheumatism
rezervace reservation
rodiče parents
rodina family
rok year
roleta blind
romantický romantic
rostlina *n* plant
rovný *adj* level
rozbitý broken (damaged)
rozdělovat se share
rozepsaný účet itemized bill
rozmrazit defrost
rozumět understand
rozvedený divorced
rtěnka lipstick
ruční flashlight
ručník towel
ruka hand (body)
rukáv sleeve
rukavice glove
ruksak backpack
růžový pink
rvačka fight (brawl)
rybník pond
rychlý quick
rychlý napřed fast (clock)
řasenka mascara
řeka river
řemesla handicrafts
řetízek chain (necklace)
řezník butcher
řidič driver
řidičský průkaz driver's license

S

s with
s titulky subtitled
sako jacket
sám alone
samoobsluha self-service (gas station); supermarket
samostatně separately
sanitka ambulance
satén satin
sauna sauna
sedadlo seat (theater)
sedadlo u okna window seat
sedativum sedative
sedět sit
sejf *n* safe
sekretářka secretary
sem here (motion)
senná rýma hay fever
servis garage (repair)
sestra sister
sestřenice cousin (female)
setkání appointment
setkat se meet
sever north
sezónní lístek season ticket
schodiště stairs
silnice road
silný strong
silný thick
sjezd exit (highway)
skákat do vody dive
skládací lehátko deck chair
sklenice glass (drinking)
skoro almost
Skotsko Scotland
skupina band (musical group)
skvělý superb
skvrna stain

slabý thin (not thick)
sladký sweet (taste)
slepé střevo appendix
sleva discount
slovník dictionary
sluchadlo hearing aid
slunce sun
sluneční brýle sunglasses
slunečník umbrella (sun)
slušet fit (clothes)
služebná maid (home)
slyšet hear
smaragd emerald
smažený fried
směnárna currency exchange office
směr direction
směrové číslo area code
snad hopefully
snadný easy
sněžit v snow
sníh n snow
snímek exposure (photos)
snubní prstínek wedding ring
socha statue
souhlasit agree
soukromník self-employed
spací pytel sleeping bag
spát sleep
speciál charter flight
specialista specialist
spěšně express
spodní prádlo underwear
Spojené Státy United States
spojení connection (train)
spojit se contact v
spokojený satisfied
společnost company (companionship);
party (social)
spolehlivý reliable

sport sport
sportovní klub sports club
sportovní potřeby sporting goods store
spravit fix
správný correct
sprcha shower
srdce heart
stadion stadium
stáhnout turn down (volume)
stan tent
stanice stop (bus)
stanice metra subway station
stanové kolíčky tent pegs
stanoviště taxíků taxi stand [rank BE]
staré město old town
starožitnost n antique
starší občan senior citizen
starý old
stát se happen
stát v cost
statek farm
státní příslušnost nationality
stavět v stop
stehno thigh
stejný same
sterilizační roztok sterilizing solution
sto hundred
strávit spend (time, money)
strojírenství engineering
strom tree
strýc uncle
střední medium (size)
střecha roof (house, car)
střevo bowel
stříbro silver
student student
studený adj cold
studovat study
stůl table

stupeň degree (temperature)
stvrzenka receipt (when paying)
styl style
suit swim
sukně skirt
suterén basement
suvenýr souvenir
sval muscle
svatba wedding
svatebná cestě honeymoon
svědek witness
svědět itch
světlo beam (headlight);
  light (electric)
světlý light (color)
svetr sweater [jumper BE]
svezení lift (hitchhiking)
svléknout se undress
svobodný single (unmarried)
syn son
synagoga synagogue

Š

šachy chess
šálek cup
šampon shampoo
šátek scarf
šatna coatroom
šaty dress
šedý gray
šek *n* check [cheque BE]
široký wide
šnorchl snorkel
šok shock (electric)
špatný bad
špička rush hour
špinavý dirty
šroubovák screwdriver
štěstí luck

štípnutí *n* bite (insect)
štípnutí komárem mosquito bite
šváb cockroach

T

tabák tobacconist
tableta pill
tábořit *v* camp
tady here (place)
také also
talíř plate
tam there
tampon tampon
tančit *v* dance
tanec *n* dance
taxík taxi
téct *v* leak (roof, pipe)
těhotná pregnant
telefon *n* telephone
telefonický hovor telephone call
telefonní budka telephone booth
telefonní číslo telephone number
telefonní karta phone card
telefonní seznam directory (telephone)
telefonovat *v* phone
tělesně postižený *adj* disabled
televize TV
tenis tennis
tenisky sneakers
tenisový kurt tennis court
tenký thin (narrow)
teploměr thermometer
teplota temperature (body)
teplý warm
terasa terrace
termoska thermos flask
těsný tight
teta aunt
tetanus tetanus

těžký difficult; heavy
tichý quiet
tlumočník interpreter
tmavý dark
toaletní papír toilet paper
topení heat
topit se drowning
tradiční traditional
tramvaj tram
trasa line (subway)
tráva grass
tričko sweatshirt
triko T-shirt
trouba oven
tržnice market
tucet dozen
tuhý hard (food)
tunel tunnel
turista tourist
turistická cesta walking route
turistická kancelář tourist office
tvrdý hard (firm)
týden week
tým team
typ *n* type
typický typical

U

u at (place); by (near)
ubrousek napkin
ubytovat se check in (hotel)
ucpaný blocked
účet bill (restaurant)
účet za telefon telephone bill
účetní accountant
učit se learn
učitel teacher
údolí valley
ucho ear

ukázat indicate
ukazatel signpost
ukradený *adj* stolen
ukrást steal
umělý synthetic
umyvadlo sink
unavený tired
uniforma uniform
upravit alter
určitě sure
ústa mouth
úsvit dawn
útes cliff
útok attack
utratit spend (waste)
uvědomit notify
uvnitř inside
uvolnit pokoj check out (hotel)
uzavírací kohout valve
úzký narrow
už already
úžasný great
úžeh sunstroke
užívat take (medicine)

V

v at (time); in (place); on
v důchodu retired
rozbít *v* break
v zahraničí abroad
vadné faulty
vaginální infekce vaginal infection
vagón car (train)
vana *n* bath
vařič stove
vařit *v* cook
včera yesterday
večer evening
večeře dinner

večírek party (event)
vědomí conscious
vedoucí manager
vegetariánský vegetarian
věk age
velikost size
Velké Británie United Kingdom
velkolepý magnificent
velký big
velmi very
velvyslanec ambassador
velvyslanectví embassy
venkovní outdoor
venkovní bazén outdoor pool
venku outside
veřejnost *n* public
vesnice village
vést *v* lead
vestibul lobby (theater, hotel)
větrák fan (ventilation)
vězení prison
věž tower
vhodný suitable
více more
víčko na čočku lens cap
video hra video game
vidět see
vidlička fork
víkend weekend
víkendová sazba weekend rate
vinice vineyard
visací zámek padlock
víta phrase
vítr wind
vitrína display window
vízum visa
vlak train
vlákno na čištění mezizubních prostorů dental floss

vlastnit *v* own
vlasy hair
vlevo left
vlhkost *n* damp
vlhký *adj* damp
vlna wave; wool
voda water
voda po holení aftershave
vodopád waterfall
vodotěsný waterproof
volejbal volleyball
volný available (free); loose
vosa wasp
vozík cart [trolley BE]
vozík na zavazadla luggage cart [trolley BE]
vpředu front (head)
vrátit return (give back)
vrátit peníze *v* refund
vrátit se return
vrchol peak
vřed ulcer
vřídek *n* boil (ailment)
vstupné admission charge
vstupní vízum entry visa
všichni all
vtip joke
vybavení equipment (sports); facilities
vybavení na turistiku hiking gear
vybitý dead (battery)
výborný good (delicious)
vyčerpaný exhausted
vyčistit clean *v*
výdej zavazadel luggage [baggage BE] reclaim
vydržet *v* last
vyfotografovat photo
vyfoukat blow dry
vyhlídka viewpoint

vycházka s průvodcem guided walk
východ east; exit; gate (airport)
vylekaný afraid
výlet excursion
výlet lodí boat trip
výloha window (store)
vyměnit cash (exchange)
vyplnit fill
vypnout turn off
vyrážka rash
vyslovit pronounce
vysoký high; tall (person)
vystrašený frightened
vyšetření examination (medical)
výška height
vyškolený trained
výtah elevator [lift BE]
vytrhnout (zub) extract (tooth)
vyvolat develop (photos)
vývrtka corkscrew
vyvrtnutý sprained
vyznání religion
vyzvednout collect
vyzvednout si pick up (something)
vyžehlit press
vzadu back (head)
vzbudit wake
vzít take (carry)
vzkaz message
vzorek specimen
vždy always

Z

z from (place)
za after (place); in (within a period of time)
zábava fun
zábavní plavba n cruise
zácpa constipation

začátečník beginner
začínat start
začít begin
záda back (body)
zadarmo free (no charge)
zadní rear
zahrada garden
zahraniční měna foreign currency
zahrnovat include
záchod restroom
záchranný člun life boat
záchranný pás life belt
zájem interest (hobby)
zájezd tour
zajímavý interesting
zalogovat log on
záloha deposit
zámek n lock
zamknout v lock
zamluvit reserve
zánět inflammation
západ west
zápach smell
zápal plíc pneumonia
zapálit v smoke
zápalky matches
zapalovač lighter (cigarette)
zápas game; match (sport)
zaplatit pay
zapnout turn on
zapomenout forget
záruka guarantee
zasnoubený engaged
zástrčka plug
zastřihnout trim
zavazadlo luggage [baggage BE]; suitcase
závažný serious
zavírat v close

závodní dráha racetrack
zavolat call (telephone)
závrativý dizzy
zavřený *adj* shut
zdravá výživa health food store
zdraví health
zdravotní pojištění health insurance
zdravotní sestra nurse
zdravotní středisko clinic
zem ground (earth)
země country (nation)
zesílit turn up (volume)
zip zipper
zítra tomorrow
zkušební kabina fitting room
zlato gold
zledovatělý.icy
zloděj thief
zlomenina fracture
zlomený broken (body part)
změnit *v* change (reservation)
změřit *v* measure
značka sign (road sign)
známka stamp
známý famous
znásilnění rape
znát know
zoo zoo
zopakovat repeat
zpáteční round-trip [return BE]
zpáteční jízdenka round trip [return BE] ticket (train)
zpáteční letenka round trip [return BE] ticket (plane)
zpěvák singer

zpoždění delay
zpráva od policie police report
zrcadlo mirror
zručnost facility
zrušit cancel
zříceniny ruins
ztratit lose
ztráty a nálezy lost-and-found [lost property BE] office
zub tooth
zubař dentist
zubní pasta toothpaste
zůstat stay (remain)
zvětšit enlarge
zvíře animal
zvláštní special
zvlhčující krém moisturizer (cream)
zvracet vomit

Ž

žádný none
žaludeční nevolnost nausea
žaludek stomach
žárovka lightbulb
žebro rib
žebřík ladder
železnice railway
žena *n* female
ženská *adj* female
žíla vein
žít live
život life
žíznivý thirsty
žláza gland